Sexuality and Discrimination

return

ISSUES

Volume 101

Editor

Craig Donnellan

Independence

Educational Publishers
Cambridge

First published by Independence
PO Box 295
Cambridge CB1 3XP
England

British Library Cataloguing in Publication Data
Sexuality and Discrimination – (Issues Series)
I. Donnellan, Craig II. Series
306.7'66

ISBN 1 86168 315 4

Printed in Great Britain
MWL Print Group Ltd

Typeset by
Claire Boyd

Cover
The illustration on the front cover is by
Don Hatcher.

CONTENTS

Introduction

Sexuality and Discrimination is the one hundred and first volume in the **Issues** series. The aim of this series is to offer up-to-date information about important issues in our world.

Sexuality and Discrimination addresses sexuality issues and looks at the legal aspects of sexuality.

The information comes from a wide variety of sources and includes:
Government reports and statistics
Newspaper reports and features
Magazine articles and surveys
Website material
Literature from lobby groups
and charitable organisations.

It is hoped that, as you read about the many aspects of the issues explored in this book, you will critically evaluate the information presented. It is important that you decide whether you are being presented with facts or opinions. Does the writer give a biased or an unbiased report? If an opinion is being expressed, do you agree with the writer?

Sexuality and Discrimination offers a useful starting-point for those who need convenient access to information about the many issues involved. However, it is only a starting-point. At the back of the book is a list of organisations which you may want to contact for further information.

*****

Exploring your sexuality

Straight, gay or bi, you don't have to label yourself immediately – or ever. However, exploring your feelings and accepting your sexuality is important

Get a grip

The most important thing is to be honest with your feelings and see where they take you. Sexuality is no easy ride; you have a whole host of emotions to get a grip of, not to mention the physical side of things.

Virtually everyone will have feelings for someone of the same sex at some stage in their life, this does not mean they have to rush out and buy a rainbow sticker for their car. It is just a natural part of sexual development. However if these feelings are more frequent or long lasting then it may be more significant.

Labels and stereotypes

Don't rush into giving yourself a label and coming out in public though. This is a very personal thing and you probably want to be comfortable with your feelings before broadcasting to your world.

Unfortunately some people can't accept any other sexual orientation to their own as being normal. They are mistaken in their thinking, and you must remember that you are not doing anything wrong or immoral. However such prejudice can, understandably, be hard to take and you may be tempted to keep your sexuality quiet. While this may seem fine in the short term, do you really want to hide this side of you forever? Be true to yourself, you have every right to be comfortable with who you are.

This is a very personal thing and you probably want to be comfortable with your feelings before broadcasting to your world

Play safe

Just because you have decided your sexual orientation does not mean you have to get jiggy with the first person you fancy. Give it time, and only get passionate when you feel ready.

Don't forget that it doesn't matter if you are gay, straight or bi – have safe sex to reduce the risk of pregnancy and getting any sexually transmitted diseases. It's also a good idea to know the law.

Find out more

You don't have to change yourself or your social life just because you have a different sexual preference to the rest of your mates. Life can tick on as normal, however it may help you to read books or articles written by or about people who have gone through the same thing as you.

You may also want to join a club or society run by gay people for gay people, it will give you support of people who understand exactly what you are going through, and will be especially helpful if you feel uncomfortable discussing everything with your mates. Although it is worth remembering that you won't necessarily like every gay person you meet, just like you don't like every straight person you meet.

■ The above information is from TheSite.org

© TheSite.org

Sexual orientation

Information from Brook

I'm a 16-year-old boy and have been having feelings for a boy in my class at school. Am I gay?

'Am I gay?' is a question that many people ask themselves when they experience feelings for someone of the same sex. It can be very daunting and scary if you feel this way. You may wonder why you feel differently to some of your friends.

It is very common to have feelings for someone of the same sex. For some people, these feelings do mean that they are gay. These people may go on to have relationships with other people of the same sex, and define themselves as gay or lesbian.

For others, these feelings may change as they develop, and they may find that they become attracted to people of the opposite sex. Other people may go on to have relationships with both men and women and define themselves as bisexual. Many people report having a crush on someone of the same sex as they grow up, or a very close loving friendship. Experiencing these feelings does not necessarily mean someone is gay. Only they can decide in their own time if this is so, as their feelings either grow or change.

All these experiences are completely normal, and only the individual concerned can reach a decision about their sexuality. It is important not to feel pressured in any way when it comes to deciding your sexuality, and to remember that there are people you can talk to for help and support if you are worried.

If you would like to talk in confidence about your sexuality, you can call the London Gay and Lesbian Switchboard 24 hours a day on 0207 837 7324.

At school I heard some of my friends talking about a friend of mine being bisexual and I think she might have heard them say this. What does this mean?

Bisexual refers to people of either sex who are emotionally and sexually

attracted to both men and women. Some people who are bisexual go through life having relationships with both men and women, while others who at first call themselves bisexual later go on to define themselves as lesbian, gay, or straight.

It is important to remember that at school rumours can fly around about people and their sexuality and that these are not always true. Your friend may be feeling upset to hear that people are talking about her behind her back and appreciate your non-judgemental support and reassurance. If your friend tells you that she is bisexual, remember that this doesn't make her any different as a friend.

Over the past few years I've realised that I'm gay. I'm terrified of telling my parents and scared they'll disown me when they find out. How can I approach them about this?

Approaching your parents about being gay can be a scary and daunting prospect, but one which will hopefully take a great weight off your mind once it has been achieved and lead to acceptance of your sexuality. There is no set easy way to approach your parents with this news, and it is best to think about what may be the most fitting way for your specific family. Some people find that it is best for them to sit their family members down together and be

---

It is very common to have feelings for someone of the same sex. For some people, these feelings do mean that they are gay

---

direct. Others wait to tell people individually, or even write their feelings down in a letter or note so that they can say exactly what they want without possible interruption.

It is important to remember that your parents will probably be shocked and confused at first, especially if they had not seen your announcement coming. They may seem angry, quiet or very upset. This does not necessarily mean that they will have a problem accepting your sexuality in the long run. Remember that your parents may have spent your life so far thinking of you and your future in a certain way, and that your announcement may challenge this. Your parents may also be upset and worried at the thought of you facing prejudice from others in society.

Talking honestly and straightforwardly about your sexuality may help your parents to cope with your news. Be prepared to answer questions they may have as this may settle some of their worries and provide them with a greater level of understanding. Time and understanding usually lead to acceptance, and most parents who learn that their child is gay continue having a close and loving relationship with their child.

I'm being badly bullied at school because I'm gay. The constant taunts are getting me down and I don't know what to do. What can I do about it?

Prejudice and ignorance are factors that cause people to bully those who seem different to the norm in the eyes of those doing the bullying. At school, young people can be cruel to others who seem slightly different from themselves.

Homophobic bullying occurs when someone is the target of verbal, physical or emotional abuse by individuals or groups because they are lesbian or gay (or thought to be by others). This bullying can cause the young person affected to feel withdrawn and depressed, with their self-esteem taking a knocking. If you are being bullied at school, it is important to remember that it is the ignorance of the people that are doing the bullying that is at fault, not you. While hard to do, standing up to the bullies and talking about your sexuality may help curb the bullying and break down the prejudices the bullies have. Talking to a teacher or parent may also help put a stop to their mean behaviour.

You do not have to suffer this bullying in silence, even if you feel unable to tell a teacher or parent. If you are a young person affected by homophobia, you can receive support and guidance on how to challenge it by calling the confidential EACH Helpline free on 0808 1000 143, Mon-Fri 9am-5pm and Sat 10am-12pm.

What is the age of consent for people who are gay and lesbian?

As with heterosexual relationships, in England and Wales it is legal for people who are gay and lesbian to have sex once both partners are 16. New law makes any touching of a sexual nature between under-16s illegal. The law applies equally to young men and women, and applies to England and Wales only.

In Scotland, it is legal for men to have sex with men if both partners are 16. There is no law about women having sex with women so provided both partners consent and are above the usual age of consent (16), it is legal.

In Northern Ireland, it is legal for men to have sex with men if they are both 17. There is no law about women having sex with women so provided both women consent and are above the usual age of consent (17), it is legal.

In Jersey, it is legal for men to have sex with men if they are both 18. There is no law about women having sex with women so provided both women consent and are above the usual age of consent (16), it is legal.

Prosecution for having sex under these ages is rare as long as both people consented and there is no evidence of exploitation or a large age difference.

I have strong feelings for my friend who is 14 just like me. Last night I even fantasised we were a couple and that she was kissing me. Is it normal to fancy someone of the same sex as me?

It is completely normal to have feelings for someone of the same sex as you, just as it is also fine to fancy someone of the opposite sex too! While you are growing up you may find you have strong feelings for women, just as for men. In fact, many people report having feelings for someone of the same sex as them at some point in life, or feeling curious as to what it may be like to be closer with someone of the same sex.

You may find that these feelings change over time and you become attracted to men, or you may find that you become attracted to other women. You may be attracted to men and women and have relationships with both. Only you can make the decision as to who you fancy in life, and it is important to remember that there is nothing wrong with being gay, straight or bisexual.

There can be a lot of pressure on someone who is uncertain of their sexuality but it is important to come to your own decision when considering your sexual identity.

If you would like to talk to someone in confidence about the feelings you are having for your friend, you can come along to one of our Brook Centres and have a chat with a counsellor. Brook Counsellors are non-judgemental and will give you space to explore how you are feeling, as well as offering support.

I'm in my first gay relationship and anxious about having anal sex. I'm not really sure what it involves.

Anal intercourse is when a man puts his penis into another person's anus and rectum. Like all aspects of sex, whether or not to have anal sex is a personal choice. Some people enjoy it, but not all men who have sex with men choose to have anal sex. With any sexual activity, it is important not to feel pressurised into doing something that you are not comfortable with.

It is completely natural to worry or feel anxious about having sex for the first time in any relationship. Deciding to become closer with someone and have sex is a big decision to make. There is a lot to think about, including whether you are ready emotionally and how to make sure that you are protected from sexually transmitted infections.

No one is expected 'to know' how to have sex if they have not done it before. Learning to feel more relaxed and confident takes time and practice. People will enjoy different experiences at different times, so what might feel good for someone might not for someone else. Sex is likely to be a more positive experience if you are able to discuss with your partner:

- what feels good for both of you
- what you are prepared to do and not do at this stage
- or any anxiety you may have about having sex for the first time
- the importance of using condoms

In any sexual relationship it is important to make sure that you use protection to protect both yourself and your partner from the risk of infections. Extra strong condoms are available for use during anal sex to protect against infection, and these can be used along with a water-based lubricant such as KY Jelly to make penetration easier. It is very important not to use oil-based products such as Vaseline as a lubricant, as these can rot the latex in condoms. Remember that some infections can be passed on though close body contact as well as penetrative sex.

I'm a lesbian, and my partner tells me that we don't need to take precautions when we have sex as we can't catch infections from each other. Is this true?
This is a myth. It is still possible to catch infections if you are in a lesbian relationship. Infections such as genital warts and pubic lice can be caught from close body contact alone, while others can be transmitted via vaginal fluids or blood. It is important to remember that some sexually transmitted infections (STIs) can be passed on through oral sex too.

To reduce the risk of infection, a condom can be used for oral sex. Dental dams (thin squares of latex) can also be used as a barrier during contact between the mouth and the vagina, or the mouth and the anus. Contact your local GUM (Genito-Urinary Medicine Clinic) for further details.

If using sex toys, these should be washed after each use. This is because some sexually transmitted infections can be passed on by sharing toys with someone else. If you use toys such as vibrators or dildos that someone else also uses, it is important to put a new condom on for each partner and activity to help reduce risk. Do not use the same sex toy for vaginal sex after using it in the anal area, as you could transfer bacteria which may cause a vaginal infection.

With lesbian, gay, and bisexual relationships it is important to protect against infections. If you are worried at any time that you may have an infection, it is important to go to a GUM clinic for a check-up. Regular testing is a good way to ensure that any potential infections can be caught quickly and treated.

My best friend has just told me she is a lesbian. I don't know how to behave around her any more. I mean, what if she fancies me?
The fact that your friend has been able to announce to you that she is a lesbian reveals how much she trusts and values you as a friend. This announcement was probably quite difficult for her to make as she may have been unsure as to how you would react.

The important thing to remember is that even though your friend has revealed something about her sexuality to you, this doesn't mean she is a changed person. She will still be the same good friend to you as she was before the announcement. If she is planning to tell other people about her sexuality, she may appreciate your support and reassurance.

Don't be afraid to ask your friend questions about her sexuality. This will help you to understand where she is coming from and also put to rest any worries or fears you have. As your friend has got up the courage to tell you about her sexuality, she is probably prepared for any questions you might have. Remember that just because your friend has told you that she is a lesbian doesn't mean she fancies you, just as straight people do not automatically fancy all their mates of the opposite sex! If this is bothering you, ask your friend.

I'm worried about my sexuality. I feel isolated and nobody I know understands what I am going through. Are there any organisations that can help me?
Yes, there are. Some people do find it helpful to explore their feelings with someone understanding and non-judgemental. You might want

to get more information and support and share your feelings with other people that have been through similar experiences.

You can contact the London Gay and Lesbian Switchboard 24 hours a day on 0207 837 7324 and talk to someone in confidence. This service acts as a source of information, support and referral to lesbians and gay men or anyone who needs to consider lesbian or gay issues. They can also signpost you to local services if this would be helpful.

Under-25s can call the GYL Project Helpline Monday-Friday between 4 and 8pm on 01656 649990. This helpline provides information, support and befriending to young lesbians, gay men and bisexuals, their families and friends.

You may also find it helpful to read about the experiences of other gay and lesbian people from the AVERT website.

If you are under 25 you can also come along to Brook and talk to a counsellor about these feelings and your concerns. A counsellor will listen and offer support. Brook counsellors are non-judgemental and won't tell you what to do. Counselling gives you the space to explore how you feel and allows you to talk about the issues affecting you.

It's the weekend, it's time to party! Is there any way I can look up what events may be happening in my area for lesbian, gay and bisexual people?
You may find it helpful to look at queery.org.uk. This is a community driven directory for lesbian, gay, bisexual and trans life. As well as listing events for the gay, lesbian and bisexual community, you can use the directory to search for voluntary and commercial services, as well as clubs, restaurants and what's on in your area. You can also find support groups and meetings in your area from this search directory.

■ The above information is from Brook's website which can be found at www.brook.org.uk Alternatively, see page 41 for their address details.
© Brook

Christianity and homosexuality

A short introduction

What is homosexuality?

A crime in the UK? No longer as long as you are over 16, don't live on the Isle of Man (21) or Channel Isles (18), and do it in total privacy (but a recent court case makes this doubtful). These restrictions only apply to males as lesbians have never figured in the law of Britain.

A disease? – No, it's not, and you can't catch it either! Homosexuals do not need medical advice any more than heterosexuals do.

A homosexual is indeed a person who is attracted physically to another of the same sex. You may believe that sex has no other dimension than producing children. But if you move beyond this narrow vision of sex, you will know that it can give a richness and a depth to relationships which are founded on love. So a lesbian or gay man is not only a sexual being, but someone seeking to give love as well as receive it.

Our understanding of many things has changed and our understanding of sex is changing too.

The Lesbian & Gay Christian Movement needs and wants to be in the vanguard of these changes.

LESBIAN ⊕ GAY CHRISTIANS

Some facts about homosexuality

Homosexuality is unusual but not unnatural. You could draw a parallel with being left-handed. A hundred years ago you would have been forced to be right-handed, but today it isn't a cause of active discrimination against you. And about one person in ten is predominantly homosexual in orientation. There are many more gay people in Britain than the whole population of Wales.

There is no real evidence to suggest that homosexuality is caused by emotional trauma, or a possessive mother, or an absent or un-sympathetic father. Some psychiatrists claim that all their homosexual patients are neurotic; but so are their heterosexual patients! Why else are they too on the couch?

High-minded moralists ask for strict laws to protect the young from homosexuals. But no greater proportion of homosexual men and women molest young children than do heterosexuals. The number is small. Some think that young people can be made into homosexuals, but no reputable psychiatrist would agree with this. What is more often needed is a friend or a counsellor to help a person clear away confusion about his or her sexual orientation. This can prevent the years of suffering and agony that people may otherwise have to endure before accepting the truth about themselves.

Can homosexuality be 'cured' or corrected'?

Young people who show 'homosexual tendencies' are often advised to get married and have a family; all will then be well, they are told. But these 'cure' marriages rarely, if ever, work and they often end in tragedy, especially for the heterosexual partner and the children. A person needs to be sure that his or her homosexual behaviour is only very superficial before even thinking of marriage.

FEAR, MYTH, IGNORANCE, BIGOTRY.

Rather, such young people need to be supported and respected in the process of trying to work through their doubts and insecurities about themselves. Without such acceptance and understanding, they may feel so threatened as to undergo extreme 'therapies', or to be 'exorcised' by misguided, albeit well-intentioned, Christians. This may temporarily change their behaviour, but dangerously blocks the facing of uncertainty which alone can lead to self-acceptance and the encouragement of responsible decisions about themselves. [These organisations are often called 'ex-gay', but they frequently avoid this term in the face of critical publicity.]

Statement of conviction

It is the conviction of the members of the Lesbian & Gay Christian Movement that human sexuality in all its richness is a gift of God gladly to be accepted, enjoyed and honoured as a way of both expressing and growing in love, in accordance with the life and teaching of Jesus Christ. Therefore it is their conviction that it is entirely compatible with the Christian faith not only to love another person of the same sex but also to express that love fully in a personal sexual relationship.

Homosexuality and the Church

Most Christians have believed and most churches have taught that you cannot be a Christian and express your love for another person of the same sex in a sexual relationship.

They believe that God has condemned this through the Bible.

We must remind ourselves of the world the people of the Bible actually lived in. Life was hard, and survival was a nation's first concern. Today, in the West, we may find it hard to comprehend the emphasis placed on child-bearing in ancient societies. In biblical times people were faced every day with basic threats to their individual and communal survival. Therefore, forms of sexuality which seemed to be at odds with the institution of the family were rejected and condemned. The law of the Jews in Christ's time illustrated this general pattern, though in other respects it

represented for its day a more careful and merciful code than the traditions of neighbouring peoples.

Christianity began as a Jewish sect; Christ was a Jew and so were all his apostles. Though the new Christian faith replaced the old Jewish law in the eyes of the early Christians, both are intimately and inextricably linked. Ancient fears about homosexuality were deeply founded in the consciousness of early Christians, whether Jewish or not, and Christianity itself certainly did not remove them.

Young people who show 'homosexual tendencies' are often advised to get married and have a family; all will then be well, they are told

---

The story of Sodom and Gomorrah is often quoted; but the real point of it is an understandable condemnation of what amounts to gang rape. It is not a condemnation of homosexual relationships as we would understand them today. It is significant that when Jesus used the story of Sodom he said that the people of that city would find the Day of Judgement easier to bear than those who refused to welcome his disciples and give them hospitality (Luke 10:11-12). And whenever else the destruction of Sodom and Gomorrah is referred to in the Bible, homosexuality isn't even mentioned.

Jesus himself said nothing about homosexuality as such, but he did teach the importance of love and commitment in relationships. He

condemned the Pharisees for keeping only to the letter of the law and for ignoring the fact that the law served a higher purpose. The Sabbath, like all of God's gifts to us, was made for us to use – with responsibility. And our sexuality is one such gift.

Paul in his letters condemned the practice of heterosexual men having intercourse with male prostitutes in pagan temples. He thought this idolatrous because human beings were used as objects of worship rather than honour being given to God. It was all destructive of love, and Paul then showed how Christ's power can rescue us from such a pattern of life if we commit ourselves to him in trust. God wants us, through Jesus, to love one another as he loved us (John 13:34).

In many respects the Church was limited by the social outlook of the times and places where the Gospel was preached. Attitudes have always changed, however slowly. Only in the last century was slavery abolished, but Paul accepted it without question. And it is only in recent times that the churches have started to examine the position of women in their own organisations and in society in general. The time is now right to have a critical look at homosexuality in a Christian context.

The Lesbian & Gay Christian Movement is not selling out on Christian truth. It is working for the very love and freedom that Christ brings to his people through his life, death and resurrection. Our Movement is working for love, for peace, for justice, and for the promotion of the Christian faith. God's work is always a struggle. Let us try to be at the heart of it.

Homosexuality today

You may have heard that somebody in your family or among your friends or at work is homosexual. Maybe it was just a whisper at a family gathering or in the canteen. Perhaps you were surprised. You might be even more astonished if the person concerned had actually told you face to face – and that is happening quite often these days.

More and more lesbian and gay people are proud to be out!

Our sexuality has far more to do with the kind of people we are and how we love others than it has to do with what happens in bed. We are no more responsible or irresponsible than anyone else. Sexual orientation has been described as 'an innocent accident'. And yet there are sections of society and the Church which either refuse to acknowledge lesbian and gay people or (perhaps worse) ignore them. Both of these attitudes are based on prejudice or lack of information, or both. Few people stop to think what it's like to be homosexual. Have you ever asked a new acquaintance 'are you married?'

There are sections of society and the Church which either refuse to acknowledge lesbian and gay people or (perhaps worse) ignore them

and received the answer, 'No, I'm gay'? Are you aware that a quarter of a million homosexuals died in Hitler's concentration camps because they were gay – and that many who survived received no compensation after the War? Do you know enough to understand homosexuality?

Do you know any lesbian and gay people?

If you think you don't, you're mistaken – their numbers are such that most people know many lesbian and gay people without realising what their sexual orientation is, and of course they include members of your family and married people.

■ The above information is from the Lesbian & Gay Christian Movement's website which can be found at www.lgcm.org.uk

© *Lesbian & Gay Christian Movement*

Transvestism and transsexualism

Transvestism and transsexualism are complex and much-misunderstood topics. Here, TheSite aims to provide a basic introduction. For more help, support and information, contact one of the organisations at the end of the article.

There is considerable prejudice displayed towards people who cross-dress or feel unhappy with their gender. It's all too easy to look for psychological disorders as a way of making sense of the issue, when the fact is there is a whole spectrum of gender and sexuality out there, and not just the fixed narrow roles to which most conform.

Here are some of the most common terms and definitions people use when discussing transvestism and transsexualism:

Gender identity
This is how people see themselves in terms of 'masculinity' and 'femininity'. These ideas are mostly shaped by the culture we live in. Gender identity is not the same thing as sexuality.

Transgender
Anyone who does not fit into the traditional male-female gender patterns of society.

Cross-dresser
Someone who wears the clothes of the opposite sex. It is done for a number of different reasons, and you should never assume that a cross-dresser is gay, bisexual or lesbian – many are heterosexual. Cross-dressers often have no desire to change their physical sex.

Transvestism
A form of cross-dressing, with the desire to adopt the clothes, appearance and behaviour associated with the opposite sex (for more info, contact the Beaumont Society. See below for details).

Gender dysphoria
This is a medical term for feeling unhappy with your current gender (masculinity/femininity), which is in conflict with your physical sex. Many of us have mild feelings like this from time to time, but some people can be tormented by gender dysphoria for years on end.

There is considerable prejudice displayed towards people who cross-dress or feel unhappy with their gender

Transsexualism
This is a strong feeling of gender dysphoria, where the person may say they are 'trapped in the body of the wrong sex'. A small proportion of transsexuals have sex reassignment surgery (a 'sex change' operation).

Intersexuality
This is where a person's physical sex is not clearly male or female. It has many causes, including chromosome syndromes or hormone imbalances. There can be a degree of gender dysphoria with it, but not always. The medical name for the condition is 'hermaphroditism', but many see this as an insulting term.

Further information
The Beaumont Trust
Advice for transgender
www.members.aol.com/Bmonttrust

The Beaumont Society
Leaflets and phonelines
www.beaumontsociety.org.uk

Gendys
Gender dysmorphia information
www.gender.org.uk/gendys/index.htm

■ The above information is from TheSite.org

© *TheSite.org*

Homosexual link to fertility genes

By Roger Highfield, Science Editor

Homosexuality is a natural side-effect of genetic factors that help women to have more children, a study suggests.

A team led by Prof Andrea Camperio-Ciani, of Padua University, found that female maternal relatives of homosexual men seemed to have more children than female relatives of heterosexual men. There was no difference with female paternal relatives.

The finding is based on a survey of 98 homosexual men and 100 heterosexual men and their relatives – 4,600 people in all.

It implies that homosexuals should be more common in societies with declining birth rates, such as Italy, where the influence of this fecundity/gay gene is more significant.

There has been much debate among scientists, based on evidence from twins and families, about why genes have evolved that seem to break the golden rule: that genes persist only because they help us to thrive and pass them on to our descendants.

Prof Camperio-Ciani said he was inspired by a conversation with his 15-year-old daughter, Georgia, who suggested that 'this interesting Darwinian dilemma' could be solved if the genetic factor linked with homosexuality could be shown to be linked also with high birth rates.

'This was a brilliant idea and I decided to test it,' he said.

Prof Camperio-Ciani, who worked with Prof Dr Francesca Corna and Dr Claudio Capiluppi, emphasises in the *Proceedings of the Royal Society, Series B* that the team's findings are based on one part of a complex interplay between genes and culture. He suggests that some genetic factors should be linked to the X chromosome (of which men carry one and women two) because

earlier work has shown how male homosexuality tends to be on the maternal, not the paternal, line.

The study by the Italian team confirmed a link with the so-called 'gay gene', Xq28, which was first identified on the X chromosome by Dr Dean Hamer in America.

It also confirmed an established theory that links homosexuality to the fraternal birth order: homosexual men are more likely to have elder brothers, but not elder sisters, than either lesbians or heterosexual men.

There has been much debate among scientists, based on evidence from twins and families

---

Prof Camperio-Ciani stressed that his study explained only 20 per cent of the variance in sexual orientation of males; otherwise homosexuality would be much more common.

'The remaining 80 per cent has yet to be understood,' he writes. 'It could – and in fact partly is – due to cultural and individual experience, or even by undiscovered biological factors.'

The Padua team speculates that the study could explain why the incidence of homosexuality appears to vary, as it did in ancient Rome where a form of condom was in use.

Prof Camperio-Ciani writes: 'When fecundity in general is high because every female reproduces as much as possible, these homosexual genes that enhance fecundity are not expressed significantly.

'But when the population is declining because of a decrease of fecundity (modern Italians) or birth control (ancient Romans), then these factors may well make the difference in relatively promoting fecundity – and therefore homosexuality – in the population.'

He adds: 'Our findings, if confirmed by further research, are only one piece in a much larger puzzle on the nature of human sexuality. Genetics is nothing without an environment to express it.'

Professor Camperio-Ciani emphasised that he had no particular axe to grind in conducting his research. 'I am very heterosexual,' he said.

© Telegraph Group Limited, London 2005

Opening doors

Facts and figures

How many lesbian, gay and bisexual people are there?

The UK Government uses the figures of 5-7% of the population, which Stonewall, the national organisation that campaigns for legal equality and social justice for lesbians, gay men and bisexuals, also feels is a reasonable estimate.

The American Alfred Kinsey's research statistics from his two studies *Sexual Behaviour in the Human Male* (1948) and *Sexual Behaviour in the Human Female* (1953), still the most extensive studies of sexual behaviour ever undertaken, also estimated those who are exclusively lesbian or gay at 6.5% of the population, which is consistent with current estimates.

Put another way, we can use these figures to estimate that every fifteenth potential user of a service for older people is a lesbian or a gay man.

At the end of the day, however, there are no hard data on the number of lesbians, gay men and bisexuals in the UK as no national census has ever asked people to define their sexual orientation – the last census, for example, only monitored same-sex couples who were cohabiting, assuming they honestly filled in the form using the term 'partner'.

Is homosexuality more common now?

Throughout history there have always been people who have had homosexual feelings and experiences. In fact, in some cultures, at some times, these feelings have been celebrated or at least accepted rather than stigmatised. However two major changes in most of Europe, America and other developed countries have taken place, which may sometimes give the impression that homosexuality is now more prevalent than at any other time:

- images of gay, lesbian and bisexual people, their lives and the issues they face have become more

visible in recent years – there are gay and lesbian characters and storylines on TV and powerful gay and lesbian images and image-makers in popular music and culture

- at the same time there have been a series of important struggles for gay and lesbian equality – in Britain this has been marked by the rights to be parents (adoptive and natural), the equalisation of the age of consent for gay men, to fair and equal treatment at work and this year the introduction of Civil Partnership for same-sex couples

These have, as has often been intended, attracted considerable media, political and legal attention, but they indicate first and foremost an increase in visibility and of rights fought for and won, rather than any increase in numbers. In other words, lesbians, gay men and bisexuals are just as numerous in older age groups, but they have on the whole simply been less visible.

Information about lesbian, gay and bisexual ageing

There is a growing body of research in the US that is allowing us to compare older lesbians, gay men and bisexuals with their heterosexual counterparts. They point to some key differences that have profound implications for service providers.

In research conducted by the Brookdale Center on Aging in New York, for example, it was found that older lesbians, gay men and bisexuals have significantly diminished support networks when compared to the general older population. Brookdale found that:

- up to 75% of older lesbians, gay men and bisexuals live alone (compared to less than 33% in the general older population)
- 90% have no children (compared to less than 20% in the general older population)
- 80% age as single people, without a life partner or 'significant other' (compared to less than 40% in the general older population)

When compared to their heterosexual counterparts, therefore, older lesbians, gay men and bisexuals are:

- $2\frac{1}{2}$ times as likely to live alone
- twice as likely to age as a single person
- $4\frac{1}{2}$ times as likely to have no children to call upon in times of need

This translates into a lack of traditional support networks that are not replaced by the strength of other close friendships or the size of informal support networks within the lesbian, gay or bisexual community, with the result that:

- 20% of older lesbians, gay men and bisexuals indicate they have no one to call on in a time of crisis or difficulty – a rate up to ten times higher than that seen in the general older population

This means that older lesbians, gay men and bisexuals are much more reliant on and have a much greater need for professional services and formal support systems in old age than is the case with their heterosexual counterparts. However, other studies in the US have shown that older lesbians, gay men and bisexuals do not access the programmes and services they need. In fact:

- older lesbians, gay men and bisexuals are five time less likely to access services for older people than is the case in the general older population, because they fear discrimination, homophobia and ignorance and that they will have to hide their sexuality

Recent history

Though the beginning of the 21st century marks an unprecedented era of positive change and progress for lesbians, gay men and bisexuals in the UK and many other countries, it is important to remember that today's older lesbians, gay men and bisexuals have lived the majority of their lives in far less liberal times. This can have a profound effect both on their preparedness to 'come out' as lesbian, gay or bisexual and the way they may view institutions and service providers – who may hitherto have been considered at best indifferent and at worst hostile until proven otherwise.

For example:

- until 1967 male homosexuality was illegal in England and Wales (until 1980 in Scotland and 1982 in Northern Ireland)
- until 1992 homosexuality for both women and men was still considered a mental disorder by the World Health Organisation
- in 1952 almost 4,000 gay men were arrested in this country simply for being gay – many went to prison and many others suffered the indignity (and often permanent physical and psychological damage) of the supposed 'cures', which included lobotomies,

aversion therapy and chemical castration
- lesbianism only escaped criminalisation ironically – to protect impressionable women: it was feared that mere mention that lesbianism existed was likely to corrupt more women than it protected

All these figures point to the fact that generic providers for older people need to make specific efforts to ensure older lesbians, gay men and bisexuals feel included, able to access services on their own terms, without fear of discrimination, and that the information and services they receive are relevant and responsive to their circumstances and needs.

Age Concern Initiatives – Opening Doors

Working with and for older lesbians, gay men and bisexuals
Opening Doors is the umbrella title of Age Concern's developing programme of publications, resources and events that seek to address the needs of the often hidden population of older lesbians, gay men and bisexuals in the UK.

The situation for most lesbian, gay and bisexual people at the beginning of the 21st century is more positive, secure and affirming than ever before. However, the majority of older people have lived a large part of their lives in less liberal times and their experience has made them understandably wary and cautious. In practice, this means that older lesbians, gay men

and bisexuals are less likely to access services and will do so on limited terms.

In addition, lesbians, gay men and bisexuals face a number of unique problems as they age, from the heterosexism of mainstream providers, who regularly assume all the older people they serve are heterosexual, to personal safety issues, to significantly diminished support networks in times of crisis. And they face serious and often distressing discrimination caused by lack of legal recognition of their relationships, not least in terms of pensions, housing, inheritance and next of kin status.

Age Concern is mindful of and warmly welcomes the important and positive benefits that will result from both the new Civil Partnership legislation and the creation of the single Commission for Equality and Human Rights. It nonetheless recognises the challenge it still faces, along with all organisations that work for the benefit of older people, in terms of fully addressing and meeting the needs of its minority communities. It is therefore committed to the promotion of good practice and to taking positive initiatives to create an environment of positive acceptance and welcome for all its lesbian, gay and bisexual clients, staff and volunteers.

- The above information is from Age Concern England's website: www.ageconcern.org.uk

© Age Concern England

A guide for young men on coming out

Do you think you might be attracted to men? Do you think you might be gay or bisexual?

Coming out . . . are you?

Coming out is the term used for the act of telling another person that you are gay or bisexual. Coming out to yourself – thinking of yourself as gay or bisexual – comes first.

For some people coming out can be straightforward, but for many it can be a confusing and stressful process. Gay and bisexual men often feel scared about coming out.

You may feel fine about coming out or you may be worried.

However you feel, we hope that you find the information in this article useful. It is intended as a starting point and will hopefully lead you on to contacting others who can support you.

Advice from people who have gone through similar experiences can make the whole process of coming out much easier for you.

> *'It was great. Mum and Dad already knew. They had been saying that I was gay since I was 8.'*
> Will, 17

There are many gay and bisexual men: some of them are famous and some are not. You do not have to try to be like any of them. There is no one correct way to be. Everyone is different, no matter who they fancy.

You are not alone. Whatever your situation, there are many organisations that can help you with your concerns and questions about coming out.

> *'I first came out as a butch lesbian. Then I realised that didn't fit. I was not a butch woman, but a transman: a female-to-male transsexual. The third time I came out was as bisexual. Finally (I hope!) I thought about my sexuality more and came out again, this time as gay. So, I'm*

> *kind of bored with coming out because I have done it so many times.'*
> Aaron, 26

Coming out . . . to yourself

Many of us have feelings for someone of the same sex. Some people may not understand this and get frightened, saying that it is bad or wrong. You may have been told that these feelings are unnatural. You may also be unsure what these feelings mean – are they friendly, romantic, or sexual feelings? Because people are anxious about same sex feelings and because feelings are complicated enough anyway, it can be difficult to come to terms with the idea that you may be attracted to men yourself. It is important that you try to accept that there is nothing wrong with you. Your sexuality is an important aspect of yourself. Accepting your feelings can be a positive experience. This may or may not mean that you start thinking of yourself as gay or bisexual. How you think about your sexuality and describe yourself is up to you.

> *'Telling people I was gay was hard, but telling myself was the hardest.'*
> Bilal, 18

Coming out is the term used for the act of telling another person that you are gay or bisexual

Coming out . . . to others
Why come out to others?
Being attracted to another man, or being gay or bisexual, is nothing to be ashamed of. In fact, if you feel very strongly about something you may want to share this with others. For example, you may have a crush on a boy and desperately want to be able to tell someone you trust. Or, you may have a new boyfriend you want to introduce to people you care about. Remember that bottling up a secret can be very difficult. You may end up having to tell more and more lies to cover up your true feelings. If you don't tell people who are close to you about your feelings, you may be cutting them off from a very important part of your life. This can make your relationships with other people very difficult just when you may need support. You may also decide that coming out may not make your relationships easier. It is up to you to decide what you want to share with other people.

> *'My parents' biggest regret was that I hadn't told them sooner. They were hurt that I was afraid to share my life with them.'*
> Mike, 20

Do I have to come out as gay or bisexual?
Your desires, fantasies and feelings are your own. It is up to you whether you want to share them with other people or not. It is also up to you to decide if you want to call yourself gay or bisexual.

If I decide to come out, who should I tell?
It's probably best to start with someone who you think will be more open and positive. Are you prepared for a bad reaction? Are you prepared for a good reaction? Talking it through first with a support worker or a telephone helpline might be helpful.

'When I came out I thought it meant I had to leave my wife, who was my best friend, and family. Instead, by being honest I was able to have a much better marriage and share my life with my best friend. I do still get some rubbish from some gay men who can't cope with me still being married.'

Adam, 33

'I became closer than I thought I could to my friends.'

Danny, 16

Should I come out in stages or all in one go?

This depends on you and how much support you have. Some people want to tell everyone at once and get it over with. Others come out over a number of years. Some people decide to tell only one or two others. Who you talk to is up to you. You may tell a close friend first or a member of your family. Remember to prepare yourself for different reactions. You are only being honest and telling someone about your feelings.

'I hated being gay and went to talk to my priest. He told my family and we prayed over me and I was sent away to be "cured". It took a while to realise this was how God made me and now I am happily married to another man. Needless to say I go to a different church.'

Luke, 23

'I told my whole family together, as I was so excited about finally realising I liked men. My family were horrified and threatened me with the police if I ever dated anyone. It took a year for them to come around and now they are brilliant.'

Sam, 29

Should I come out to my parents?

Whether you have a close relationship with your parents or not, you may feel that this is an important part of your life that you want to share with them. Some people find it easier to discuss the subject with one parent or another member of the family first before approaching the rest of the family. Other people decide not to discuss their sexuality with their families. It is up to you.

Do you have the telephone number of a gay switchboard or parents' organisation that could help you or your parents?

'I told my mother after my friends and she felt hurt that I hadn't told her first.'

Steven, 25

Coming out . . . how to do it

There is no right place or right time or right way to come out. It is best to try to avoid an argument about it, and of course it is best not to do it when you've had too much to drink. Try to plan ahead.

When coming out to someone, remember how long it has taken you to accept your sexuality. Others may need time to accept this also – so try to keep calm.

Here are some suggestions for responses to statements some people might make:

It's just a phase.
Things may change in the future, but this is how I feel now. And that is what is important.

It's not important.
It is to me. I've had to build up a lot of courage to tell you.

Was it something I did?
No. It's just the way I feel.

God says it is wrong.
God made me the way I am.

Now it's said, don't mention it again.
If I don't, I will have to lie about where I've been and who I see. I'm not willing to do that.

Why do you have to tell everyone about what you do in bed?
I'm not. I'm talking about my sexuality, which is different from sex. I'm telling you about me.

'I told me parents I was gay when I was 16. They threw me out and put an announcement in our community paper saying I was dead. It took 10 years before they would speak to me again.'

Ahmed, 29

'It was much harder coming out in my 50s and explaining to so many people who thought they knew me that they didn't. My wife was really angry and hurt, but my children did try hard to understand. My wife still finds it hard but we are working on our friendship.'

John, 59

■ The above information is from *Coming out . . . a guide for young men,* produced by Healthy Gay Scotland. See page 41 for their address details.
© *Healthy Gay Scotland*

Coming out

Information from *PS Magazine*

Thoughts and feelings of isolation, loneliness, shame and suicidal tendencies are evident in the life of many young, gay teenagers. Although now I am totally open about my sexuality, the coming out process was difficult, initially filled with feelings of resentment but then of acceptance and eventually love. Coming out to your family and friends can make you more comfortable with your sexuality and happier with yourself as a person. This is my life.

I didn't 'come out' to my parents; I had the unfortunate experience of being 'found out'. Although this wasn't my intention, I had been continually lying to my parents about where I was spending the night, and who I was spending it with.

The revelation of my homosexuality came as a sharp, dramatic shock to my parents and their reaction was clearly a reflection of the way in which they found out. From here on, no part of my life could be the same: my friendships, my schooling or my family. I was in school completing my A-levels, totally unaware of what lay ahead of me. It was around this time that I formed a close bond with a member of my class. In the short space of time that I knew him, he dramatically revealed his sexual orientation and his attraction to me over the phone one night. Clearly shocked, stunned and put out – I told him that his feelings were reciprocated and as a result we started to date.

Unknown to me, in the summer holidays a group of people from my school saw me out with my boyfriend, K. Although we weren't holding hands or kissing, it was clear that we were a couple. A few days later, I had been 'Outed'. Some of my friends took to the situation badly; I lost quite a few of the people I cared about. This period proved to be testing to my beliefs, my personality and myself. Still clearly wounded from traumatic relationships, I got to the stage where I couldn't cope. My school work was suffering, I couldn't sleep, for a period of time I was a shell of my former being – until I decided no more. I spoke to my form tutor about bullying, the taunts and the jibes – I was clear, concise and direct. I took charge of my life, and as a result the school bullying stopped.

Although now I am totally open about my sexuality, the coming out process was difficult, initially filled with feelings of resentment but then of acceptance and eventually love

---

I was able to grow as a person, learn more about my parents and myself, and be able to let myself love and be loved by another gay teenager.

I am now happy with my sexuality and am ready to continue my gay life. I was also able to grow from this experience and learn from my mistakes. I was finally able to become free from the illusion I had lived with all of my life.

In terms of coming out, my advice for any gay person is to wait

until you feel it's right to tell the people you love – don't feel pressurised or under any sort of time constraint. I seem to grow through every setback; every tear makes me stronger, more connected to the real James. Yet the past two years also symbolise feelings of anger, hatred, rejection, missed opportunities and feelings of incredible loneliness. Through failed and very often turbulent relationships, family arguments, temporary homelessness and a friend's HIV scare; I am a new person. Remember that, whatever happens to you and your life, there is always someone to talk to, someone who cares and someone who loves you for who you are, no matter what creed, race or sexuality.

My advice to any lesbian/gay or bisexual person out there is to find out who you are – love yourself for it and never listen to any people who ridicule you or put you down. You are an amazing and diverse individual, who doesn't necessarily have to live their gay life as a stereotype, I don't and it makes me happy and content with who I am. Concentrate on the positive things in your life, join a youth group – find someone you trust and talk through your feelings, talk about the fears and the fun times.

The future for me will be filled with love, ambition and respect for myself as I finally feel that like a caterpillar, once I was troubled with my former 'straight' self with the loneliness and anger I felt and yet now I have now emerged from my cocoon (or closet) to become a butterfly. Only now this butterfly has rainbow coloured wings! And also – yes I like Will Young! :-)

■ The above information is from *PS Magazine* published by the Peer Support Project. For more information visit their website at pspcore.org.uk/index.php

A guide for families and friends of lesbians and gays

Information from Families and Friends of Lesbians & Gays (FFLAG)

Beginning to understand

Many books have been written, much has been said and many theories have been advanced about homosexuality, but from all this, only one fact emerges: no one has conclusively proved what it is that causes homosexuality; and yet, unhappily, and wrongly, homosexuals are discriminated against.

The weight of evidence increasingly suggests that homosexuality is genetic. That is, just as random genetic pattern dictates that one member of a family may be blond haired or left handed, so a similar random pattern in the genes will produce a lesbian or gay orientation. However, this and other theories are of little help to people, particularly parents, faced with the news that a person they love may be lesbian or gay.

To explain homosexuality in simple terms is not an easy thing. Basically, it is a whole emotional pattern, present from early years, which the child develops as he or she matures. It need have no effect on their lives beyond the fact that their deepest relationships will be formed with people of their own sex. Like all of us, lesbian and gay people want and need to give love and to have

that love returned. Lesbian and gay people can relate to others who are not homosexual in every way, except sexually. In sex itself, lesbians and gay men are no different from the rest of the population; some have a great interest in sex, others have very little interest, and most are somewhere in between.

Not an illness

The question is often asked, 'can this condition be cured?' The answer is that homosexuality is not an illness. It is a natural state of affairs for lesbian or gay people. They do not choose this any more than anyone else chooses to be heterosexual. Sexual orientation, whether homosexual or heterosexual is not of our making and we are not responsible for the reason or process of creation.

Not chosen

It cannot be repeated often enough that sexual orientation is not chosen,

that instead, it is an emotional pattern present from the beginning which develops as the child grows. As with all children, sexual awareness comes as the body develops. At this point, it is very important to make a distinction between a lesbian or gay experience, which many children have, and lesbian or gay orientation.

The first is sexual play, a purely physical experiment without any emotional involvement; the second is a complete way of relating and involves very deep emotional experiences.

Early difference

It is, however, at this early stage of sexual awareness, that the lesbian or gay child first feels different; first feels attracted emotionally and sexually to the same sex. In the present climate of hostility, discrimination and prejudice, and perhaps in fear and confusion, a son or daughter will often deny their sexual orientation, even to themselves.

A daughter or son who feels that they are of lesbian/gay orientation, has probably been consciously aware of those feelings since the age of 11 or 12. Such people, recalling

this period, usually talk of a growing feeling of uneasiness, of feeling apart from other children in a way they cannot quite understand.

Stress and identification

The conflict and lack of identity, the feeling of isolation and guilt they have been taught to have, often results in great distress. Regretfully, current society still focuses on the assumption that only heterosexuality is the accepted norm, although progress to equality continues to be made.

As their sexual development speeds up, it becomes clear that this difference is a sexual one. These children are often overtaken by fear and loneliness. They do not necessarily identify with the lesbian and gay people portrayed on television, even though this image has improved in recent years, and attempts are now made by producers and playwrights to depict more accurate lifestyle characters and programmes for the quite sizeable lesbian and gay audiences.

Rejection and ridicule

Gay and lesbian young people fear rejection by their parents, and possibly by anyone else they might turn to for guidance. They fear scorn, or even aggression, from their friends or classmates, some of whom may be repeating the sort of 'queer' jokes that abound in school playgrounds, and, regretfully, amongst some older people.

They fear they might give themselves away with a look, a glance, or even an untimely remark. They experience great difficulty in meeting other lesbian/gay people and, in isolated circumstances, can feel 'they are the only lesbian/gay person in the world' to quote a phrase we have often encountered. In short, lesbian and gay young people feel exactly the same sense of shock and fear that parents encounter when faced with this knowledge of their daughter's or son's orientation. They face it alone. It is not uncommon for a young lesbian/gay person to spend three or four years summoning up enough courage to talk to their parents.

Ignorance

If we examine the reasons for these varying reactions, a fairly consistent pattern emerges. Firstly, although there are some well-written books concerning lesbians and gays, they tend not to be well known, and are not always stocked by public libraries or booksellers. Secondly, parents, in common with the rest of society, have absorbed all the myths and misunderstandings which exist about homosexuality.

Little information exists for the parents of a lesbian/gay child. Very rarely, if at all, does the subject of homosexuality get talked about in the home or socially other than in a 'media sensational' sense, and then usually in a very biased way based upon limited knowledge or distorted by the media. The image, which you then have, may be very little different from that which you first learned in the playground, in an atmosphere of prejudice, fear and ridicule towards homosexuality. Even parents who consider themselves to be very understanding on this matter do not expect it in their own family. Do not feel guilty. These prejudices, these misunderstandings and misconceptions, are prevalent in our society. They are not ideas that you as parent, family or friend of a lesbian/gay person decide to have. As you gain more information and the shock lessens, you will find, slowly, that they will pass, as you realise how distorted and prejudiced these images are, and how much discrimination against homosexuals they are responsible for.

Parents' reaction

For parents, totally unprepared for this development in their child, the general reaction is one of shock, bewilderment and fear. Some blame themselves, some reject the child, some want to help but do not know how to cope. Many, in spite of themselves, feel alienated from their own child. Even where love maintains the bond, this does not lessen the shock and the confusion parents feel.

Religious prejudice and intolerance

Thirdly, if parents hold certain religious beliefs, one of the difficulties they may experience is in reconciling these doctrines with the lesbian/gay orientation of their daughter or son. It is not possible in this article to reach for, or to offer, a solution that would be acceptable. However, a few pointers can be given.

Gay and lesbian young people fear rejection by their parents, and possibly by anyone else they might turn to for guidance

---

A very great deal of work is being done by clergy of all denominations to bring a more tolerant attitude towards lesbian/gay persons.

The laws of the Church are based generally upon the old Hebraic laws, and whilst it may have been necessary at that time for the Jewish people to 'be fruitful and to go forth and multiply' for the sake of their survival, this is certainly not the case today when we need population limitation. The writings attributed to St Paul, for instance, were written nearly two thousand years ago and, however valid they may or may not have been at that time, it is very doubtful whether some of the discriminatory strictures on sex in general that he supposedly expressed, would be acceptable in the light of present knowledge. We are taught that 'we are all God's children' and many lesbian/gay people are committed believers. For people holding other religious beliefs the problem is undoubtedly more difficult, and for them it would be best to refer to the counselling advice that is given by the appropriate religious organisations.

Choices

Parents quite often use the phrase 'Why did my child choose this way of life?' It must again be emphasised that a lesbian/gay orientation is not chosen, it is natural to the person. In view of the many difficulties with which lesbians and gays have to cope, and the hostility that they will probably face, even from those who know and love them, it must surely be abundantly clear that most people would not go out of their way to choose a way of life so fraught with possible pressures. People do not choose to be heterosexual. It is simply part of them. It is exactly the same for lesbians and gay men.

Similarly, parents often ask, 'Where did I go wrong?' This is only an issue if being lesbian or gay is thought to be a 'problem'. They have not gone wrong. There is nothing that they have done, or failed to do, that made their child lesbian/gay.

Parents' organisations

Since 1969, parents' organisations have dealt with many thousands of families from every strata of society – 'average' families, families that have faced divorce or separation, single-parent families, families of ethnic minorities or of mixed race, families where independence is the norm, large families, small and single-child families, nuclear families, extended families, families undergoing great strain, and families with little difficulty.

Parents' organisations are thus in a unique position to see any common factor; any factor in background, upbringing, environment, children's or parents' attitudes or experiences that causes homosexuality. None has been found. Instead, the experience of parents' organisations has been that the explanations commonly offered for the existence of lesbian/gay people hold little logic.

Myths around parents' 'fault'

Take, for example, one of the most widespread explanations, that a weak or absent father and a strong, dominant mother will produce a gay son – something which is clearly untrue. Were it true, it would mean that the Second World War, when millions of men were absent from home for considerable periods, would have resulted in a huge increase of lesbians and gays amongst the children who were born and grew up

---

Some parents speak first

Just occasionally, parents will recognise their child is lesbian/gay before their child has the courage to approach them. What lesbian/gay children generally say is that, for them, the easiest way for the subject to be brought up would be if their mother or father were to say something like the following: 'I've felt for a while you might be lesbian/gay. If you are, I want you to know that it makes no difference to the love I feel for you. I will need to find out more about the subject so that I can know how best to help you lead a happy life. Whether you are lesbian/gay or not, I love you, and, if it helps, let's talk about things.'

These thoughts, however phrased, and in some families they might be better written than spoken, can provide a bridge to the child who may be anxious to talk, but is unable to find the words. Even young people, who clearly know they are lesbian/gay, can have difficulty in accepting this side of them. Thus, it can be better to gradually and gently restate, over a period of time, your love for your child and the strength of that bond, so creating an atmosphere in which it is easier for your son or daughter to talk.

---

at that time: something that did not occur. What these and other theories are really saying, without having the courage to say it outright, is that the parent is to blame for having a lesbian/gay child.

Try to see how untrue this is. If you have other children, ask yourself if there was anything different in the way you brought up this child than the way you brought up the others. If you have only one child, ask yourself if his or her upbringing was so dramatically different to that of other children. It is unlikely. Even if something in this son or daughter's background has been so markedly different, why, of all the thousands upon thousands of consequences this could have had, should it have resulted in lesbian/gay orientation?

The truth is that it is easier for parents to seek faults in themselves than to face the fact that there is a side to their child that they never knew about. This search for a cause inside yourself is a punishment you are inflicting upon yourself. It will help neither you nor your child. Indeed, you are actually increasing the problems of your daughter or son by such agonising.

People do not choose to be heterosexual. It is simply part of them. It is exactly the same for lesbians and gay men

---

Family strength

Try to accept the fact that you have had a shock for which few parents are prepared. Your child, gradually over a period of years, has had the same shock. Now put some faith in the strength that family relationships can have in a time of crisis. Recognise that there is no 'right' or correct way for parents to react in this situation. As in all family situations, however you would have reacted until now, your child will need a signal that you still love him or her, no matter what. Whether this is done in words or deeds, it is the start of getting things right.

Emotions are all right

Do not smother your emotions with reason. Some parents will say they have come to terms and that they accept this is the way their child is, even while feeling deeply upset inside. Do not deny your emotions. It is better to tell your child that this was a shock you were totally unprepared for, that you still love him or her and nothing has changed that, but you still need time to let the shock run its course and to get support, such as that offered by FFLAG. Meanwhile, get in touch with a parents' organisation with the aim of not only getting information and support, but to express your feelings. Parents feel shock, hurt and guilt as much as anyone else. Expressing these feelings to someone outside the family, who nonetheless understands, will greatly reduce the burden you feel, and lessen the risk of confrontation in the family.

Bisexual

Parents often ask if their child will change as he or she grows older, and whether it will be too late should the realisation come that he or she is not predominantly homosexual after all – will great emotional damage have been done? The answer is that it is not possible to speak for all children in all circumstances.

If the child is in his or her early teens, there is always the possibility that they are bisexual, although practising bisexuals are a small proportion of the population and these feelings are natural to them. Given the pressure that a young lesbian/gay person faces, it is unlikely that someone who is not of this orientation would for long believe that they were. What is far more important is that they should not be pressured. The support, love and understanding of parents and those closest are vital at this very difficult time of life.

Not paedophiles

Another misconception that some parents have is that lesbian/gay persons want to have sexual relations with very young children. This is totally untrue. It is one of the myths that have grown out of the ignorance of society about the nature of homosexuality. The normal, adjusted lesbian/gay person has no more interest in young children sexually than does the normal adjusted heterosexual. Indeed, statistics prove quite conclusively that the greatest amount of child abuse sexually is committed by heterosexuals, and, most regrettably, occurs within the family.

It's not unusual

Another very common question is: 'Are there more lesbian/gay persons now than there used to be?' Figures used in the pre-1957 Wolfendon Report showed that at least one in twenty of the population is predominantly or exclusively lesbian or gay. More recent surveys show that the proportion is far more likely to be around one in fifteen. This is not an increase, it is simply that since a measure of decriminalisation, like the 1967 Act, more people have felt freer to 'come out' or be visible. This is

particularly true of young people. They are increasingly unprepared to live on two levels: to be one person in the home and another outside of it. This is one of the reasons why so many now tell their parents. If the quoted figures of lesbian/gay statistics are considered, does it not mean that homosexuality could occur in any family? Therefore, this is not a situation in isolation.

The family, we are frequently told, is the very fabric of our society. We may be personally involved with lesbian and gay people in our families, at work or in our social lives. In any of these settings, lesbians and gay

HIV and AIDS

Finally, and very importantly, the fears of parents, relatives, friends and associates about HIV/AIDS must be faced. The one very positive step parents can take, and should take, is to ensure that their children, whether lesbian/gay or heterosexual, have a full knowledge of this subject and are aware that in all sexual intercourse involving vaginal, oral or anal contact 'safe sex' must be practised. This means using a sheath (condom). It should be a priority to make literature available for them. This cannot be over-emphasised, since the disease is transmitted via contact with semen, blood, or body fluids. As in all sexual matters, knowledge dispels risk and fear. Ignorance and prejudice can be, quite literally, killers. Make sure that you are fully aware.

men need our understanding, our support, our respect and our love. This comes from knowledge. Discrimination comes from ignorance.

Partner

If a lesbian or gay person brings their partner home for acceptance and hospitality, they should be given the same welcome that would be extended to the partner of a heterosexual member of the family.

This stage may take some time to reach, and love and respect are the means by which it will happen, but it is necessary to recognise the need to overcome prejudice in the interests of all, and particularly in order for you to continue to give the warm welcome which is every child's right, and which, if you freely give, will be given to you in return.

Conclusion

We have tried, above all, in this article to emphasise that homosexuality is a state of being, just like heterosexuality. It is very difficult to become a full happy human being if your sexuality is being denied, particularly by those who love or have regard for you. By sharing in a part of this person's life, you will be helping to strengthen the bonds between you, and greatly raise everyone's chance of happiness.

■ The above information is from Families and Friends of Lesbians & Gays' (FFLAG) website which can be found at www.fflag.org.uk

© Families and Friends of Lesbians & Gays (FFLAG)

Teachers told to promote Gay Pride

By Laura Clark

Schools are being urged to advertise gay lifestyles to children in a Government drive to 'challenge homophobia'.

In an attempt to clamp down on supposedly homophobic language, the guidelines say teachers should be reported if they refer to boys as 'sissies', accuse them of standing around 'like a mothers' meeting' or call them a 'bunch of girls'.

Staff are asked to put up flyers for Gay Pride marches and Mardi Gras festivals. They are told that promoting a 'positive stance' on homosexuals and lesbians can help tackle homophobic bullying.

The guidance, which applies to all ages from nurseries upwards, drew a furious response from Church leaders and family campaigners who said it went too far.

The booklets, which were sent to every local education authority this month, also urge schools to:

- invite in gay visitors and speakers to act as 'sexual minority role models' where there are no homosexual members of staff;
- keep written records of every homophobic phrase used, either by staff or pupils;
- form a 'homophobia working party' to increase awareness of homophobic bullying;
- teach pupils about homosexual public figures such as MPs and entertainers;
- avoid generic language that assumes parents and staff always have partners of the opposite sex.

Local education authorities are expected to make the guidance known to all schools in their area.

Heads and teachers can also download the resources titled *Stand Up For Us: Challenging Homophobia in Schools* from Government websites.

Pupils of all ages

Schools are urged to 'normalise sexual minorities' by putting up information on gay and lesbian issues in corridors and waiting areas. Staff are told never to leave unchallenged any homophobic language, including the use of 'gay' as a generic insult.

The booklet gives the example of a pupil who describes a classmate's trainers as 'so gay'. It makes clear that the guidance is targeted at pupils of all ages – even those at nurseries.

'The issues and practical approaches outlined in this resource

> *Schools are urged to 'normalise sexual minorities' by putting up information on gay and lesbian issues in corridors and waiting areas*

apply equally to early years settings, primary, secondary and special schools, off-site units and pupil referral units.'

The guidance prompted renewed concerns over the influence of the gay lobby following the repeal last year of Section 28 – the law which banned the promotion of homosexuality in schools.

'Heavy-handed'

Norman Wells, director of the pressure group Family and Youth Concern, said: 'This is part of a radical social agenda which will only cause more confusion among vulnerable young people and expose them to increased risk to their physical and emotional health.

'The overwhelming majority of parents opposed the repeal of section 28 precisely because they feared this kind of aggressive promotion of homosexuality.'

The Reverend Rod Thomas, of the conservative Church of England Reform movement, said: 'Church schools would have a huge amount of difficulty with this and I don't think any would feel at ease promoting a Gay Pride event.

'This takes anti-discrimination measures too far into the realm of positive discrimination.'

A spokesman for the Tories said: 'This campaign does appear heavy-handed.'

The guidance was produced jointly by the Department for Education and Department of Health.

A spokesman for the Education Department said: 'It is up to teachers to use their professional judgment in deciding what resources and strategies to adopt.'

■ This article first appeared in *The Daily Mail*, 24 December 2004.

'Pride Not Prejudice' reveals hidden bullying

Information from YWCA

YWCA England & Wales is calling on schools and the government to act now to put an end to hidden bullying that is leaving young women isolated, lonely and in fear, and in some cases driving them from the classroom.

In its latest briefing, *Pride not Prejudice: young lesbian and bisexual women*, YWCA urges schools to ensure that bullying of young lesbian and bisexual women is included in anti-bullying policies and to enforce a zero tolerance attitude to such behaviour amongst teachers and pupils.

> *'I used to get pelted with stones to and from school. I ended up being pinned against a wall and got stabbed.'*
>
> Kath, 20

Previous research and recent interviews conducted by YWCA with young women who are lesbian, bisexual or questioning their sexuality identified severe verbal or physical abuse in school as a major issue and one which teachers find it difficult to confront. Subsequent research by YWCA into how many schools are tackling the issue revealed that less than 15 per cent of schools mention bullying relating to sexuality in their anti-bullying policies, despite government guidelines recommending that the issue be addressed.

137 schools responded to the YWCA survey. All have anti-bullying policies, but only 13 per cent have policies which mention bullying relating to sexuality. This shows very little difference to similar research in 1997, which revealed that six per cent of schools addressed homophobia in their policies.

Steph Green, Director of Services to Young Women at YWCA, said: 'Policies alone won't solve bullying in schools, but they are the foundation on which to build a strategy. If bullying relating to sexuality isn't even mentioned in anti-bullying policies, how can a young woman expect to feel safe if she is "coming out" as lesbian or bisexual? Every young woman – regardless of her sexual identity – has the right to live, learn and work in a safe environment free from fear, intolerance and prejudice. Society is letting these young women down.'

A number of schools showed very good practice, with compre-

> *'I found myself in the playground, with 30 or 40 kids surrounding me, shouting at me. Not one single teacher came and intervened.'*
>
> Sam, 18

hensive policies tackling all forms of bullying. However, there was a lack of consistency, even within individual Local Education Authorities.

Ms Green continues: 'Our interviews with young women showed just how vulnerable they can be when discovering their sexuality. Many face severe isolation and serious emotional problems because there is no one they can turn to. They face a brick wall just when they need the most support. One young woman told us how she was being openly harassed in class. When she asked her teacher to intervene, he simply told her to get on with her work. The next day he left a note of apology on her desk, but still he said nothing to the other pupils and the bullying continued.'

Ben Summerskill, Chief Executive of Stonewall, said: 'We welcome YWCA's informed and well-resourced briefing *Pride not Prejudice*. It not only gives an overview of the issues facing young lesbian and bisexual women but also gives useful recommendations for future action.'

Where bullying occurs

Research suggests that most teachers are aware of homophobic bullying in their school. The table below shows where the bullying is likely to take place

Type of bullying	Corridors	Classrooms	School grounds	Changing rooms	On the way home	Other places
Called names	xxx	xxx		x		x
Teased				x		
Hit/kicked			xx		xx	
Frightened by look/stare	x	xx		xx	xx	x
Rumour-mongering	xx			x		
Public ridicule	xx	xxx	xx	x	x	
Sexual assault				x		
Belongings taken			x	x		

xxx = frequently; xx = regularly; x = sometimes

Source: (Rivers, 2000) Stand up for us, DFES, DoH. Crown copyright 2004

'Sex education is another big issue. How was I supposed to know how to have safer sex when lesbian sex wasn't even mentioned in sex and relationships education? I had no idea what I could or couldn't catch. and that scared me for a long time.'

Sam, 18

Pride not Prejudice explores many of the issues faced by young women as they discover their sexuality, including the difficulties of 'coming out' to family and friends; discrimination and prejudice within the health service; violence; sexual abuse and a lack of relevant sex and relationships education. Key recommendations include:

- All schools' anti-bullying policies should explicitly include bullying on the grounds of sexuality

- Schools should exercise a zero tolerance attitude towards homophobic bullying and promote tolerant attitudes towards lesbian, gay and bisexual lifestyles
- Sex and relationships education should incorporate issues of questioning sexuality, coming out, lesbian and gay relationships and lesbian and gay health, including safer sex
- Local authorities and voluntary organisations should provide space and resources for lesbian and bisexual young women's groups
- The government should place a positive duty on all public bodies to promote equality on the grounds of sexuality, as is currently the case on the grounds of race
- The health service should tackle discrimination against its workers and clients. Practitioners, such as doctors and nurses, should not make assumptions about sexuality and they should guarantee young women's confidentiality and offer support to them.

'I'm okay now, finally. Getting away from school, getting a job and being in a steady relationship has made the difference.'

Sam, 18

- The above information is from YWCA's website which can be found at www.ywca.org.uk

© YWCA

It's official – discrimination affects our health

A study has just been published by the *British Journal of Psychiatry*, claiming that homophobia is to blame for high rates of mental health problems amongst lesbian, gay and bisexual people.

This has long been the opinion of agencies such as the Lesbian and Gay Foundation and Stonewall, but it's the first time that a study has examined the potential effect of discrimination on the mental health of the LGB community.

The survey asked 1,285 lesbian, gay and bisexual people various questions about their mental health and some disturbing results were found such as:

- A massive 83% of respondents said that they had experienced some form of hate crime in the previous five years, including damage to property, personal attacks or verbal insults and most felt that this was due to their sexuality.
- 40% of respondents had suffered from problems such as anxiety, panic attacks, depression, sleep disturbance, problems with

memory or concentration, compulsive behaviour or obsessive thoughts.
- Around the same number also reported periods of self-harming.

The report recognises that homophobia takes place in all parts of people's lives and can start as early as school with LGB children being bullied.

It seems that that is where the answer lies. If we are to overcome this problem we need to educate people from a very early age about the damaging effects of homophobia and we need to provide LGB children with more support throughout their education.

If you have suffered as a result of homophobia, it's important that you don't suffer in silence. The Lesbian and Gay Foundation offers a full counselling service and there is a police surgery available at our headquarters every Thursday night.

Or for more information on how you can get support go to: www.report-it.org.uk

- The above information is from *outnorthwest magazine*, published by the Lesbian and Gay Foundation. For further information, visit their website which can be found at www.lgf.org.uk

© Lesbian and Gay Foundation

Equal at school

Information from Stonewall

Real issues, real lives . . .

'If you're gay, you don't admit to it. There's this one boy who gets bullied all the time now, not because he is gay, it's more about his appearance, he's more feminine, has a higher voice. People call him names like "bent". No one in the school would admit to being gay. No one would be strong enough to come out with it.'

Year 11 pupil, mid Glamorgan

The issues

For young lesbians, gay men and bisexuals, being equal at school means getting on with their lives and their studies without facing bullying or harassment, in the classroom or in the playground, because of their sexuality. There is considerable evidence that homophobic bullying is widespread in schools. There is also evidence that section 28 has left a legacy that makes it harder to tackle homophobic bullying. Section 2A of the 1996 Local Government Act (Scottish equivalent of section 28 in England and Wales) was repealed in Scotland in 2000, but the vitriolic campaign leading up to its repeal left teachers scared and wary of discussing issues relating to homosexuality. On 10 July 2003 the House of Lords supported the earlier decision of the House of Commons and voted to repeal section 28 in England and Wales. On 18 September 2003 the Local Government Bill received Royal Assent and Section 28 was finally to be taken off the statute books.

The law

The Children Act 1989 requires that 'the needs and concerns of gay young men and women must also be recognised and approached sympathetically'.

Section 28 of the Local Government Act 1988 stated that no local authority shall 'promote the acceptability of homosexuality as a pretended family relationship'.

On 21 June 2000 the Scottish Parliament overwhelmingly passed the Ethical Standards in Public Life Bill, which included the repeal of the equivalent of section 28 in Scotland, by 99 votes to 17. England and Wales were the only countries in the world with a law like section 28, and now it is finally repealed.

Many people thought that schools in England and Wales could not talk about sexuality or deal with homophobic bullying because of section 28. However section 28 did not apply to schools and did not prevent schools from addressing issues of sexuality or homophobic bullying. The following guidance governs the regulation of sex education in English schools. DfES

Circular 1988 states that 'section 28 does not affect the activities of school governors or teachers . . . does not prevent objective discussion on homosexuality nor counselling. . .' Additionally, the Local Government Act 2000 Section 104 reads 'nothing in section 28 . . . shall be taken to prevent the head teacher or governing body of a maintained school, or a teacher employed by a maintained school, from taking steps to prevent any form of bullying'.

The Learning & Skills Act, dealing with sex education in maintained schools, was passed at the end of July 2000. The Act clarifies that a) local authorities have no responsibility for sex education b) no inappropriate materials should be used in the teaching of sex education and c) materials should take account of a pupil's age, cultural and religious beliefs.

New Sex and Relationship Education Guidance was published in July 2000. This statutory guidance has a section dealing with the needs of young lesbians, gay men and bisexuals – the first time ever gay sexuality has been recognised – which requires schools to deal with homophobic bullying. Section 1.30 states: 'It is up to schools to make sure that the needs of all pupils are met in their programmes. Young people, whatever their developing sexuality, need to feel that sex and relationship education is relevant to them and sensitive to their needs.' Section 1.32 states: 'Schools need to be able to deal with homophobic bullying.' Similar guidance was produced for Scottish schools as part of the package of support surrounding the repeal of section 28 and the Standards in Scotland's Schools Act 2000 places a duty on schools to develop an annual equality action plan.

DfES 2002 anti-bullying pack for schools *Bullying: Don't Suffer in Silence* recommends including homophobic bullying in the school's anti-bullying policy 'so pupils know discrimination is wrong and the schools will act'. It also suggests covering homophobic bullying in INSET, guaranteeing confidentiality and appropriate advice, dealing with homophobic language and exploring issues of diversity and difference.

More recently, DfES 2004 *Stand up for us: challenging homophobia in schools* offers practical advice on responding to homophobic bullying, auditing the problem and supporting pupils and staff.

The drawing up of sex education guidance for Welsh schools is a matter for the National Assembly for Wales. In July 2002 for the first time the Welsh Assembly Government's new Sex and Relationships in Schools Guidance states that issues of sexuality and sexual orientation should be dealt with honestly, sensitively and in a non-discriminatory way.

The problem

Although section 28 is gone now, it has created a climate of fear and abuse which teachers are either unaware of or feel powerless to deal with.

A 1999 survey found that, out of 1,000 Stonewall supporters, 77% had been bullied at school. A 1997 study by the Institute of Education found that 61% of teachers surveyed were aware of lesbian, gay or bisexual pupils in their school and 42% of teachers had been asked personal advice on lesbian, gay and bisexual issues by their pupils. Yet 57% of schools reported that they did not have information relating to sources of support for lesbian, gay and bisexual pupils and 51% reported at least one incident of homophobic bullying in the last term. 99% of surveyed schools have general anti-bullying policies but only 6% had specific anti-homophobic provisions.

It is clear that young lesbians, gay men and bisexuals or those perceived to be lesbian, gay or bisexual, experience high levels of abuse and violence and that these experiences are damaging. In a study in 2000 by Ian Rivers, *Social inclusion, absenteeism and sexual minority youth*, 72% of young lesbians, gay men and bisexuals indicated that they had either

played truant or feigned illness to avoid homophobic abuse at school, 40% had attempted suicide on at least one occasion, and 36% of those persistently absent reported multiple episodes of self-harm.

Stonewall campaigns

Stonewall was set up in 1989 after section 28 was first passed and fought for its repeal for over 10 years. Stonewall successfully campaigned for the House of Commons and the House of Lords to vote for an amendment to the Local Government Bill 2003 that repealed section 28 in England and Wales.

Anti-gay groups frequently say that section 28 was used to manage teaching about gay issues in schools. This is incorrect. Section 28 never applied directly to schools, it in fact applied only to local authorities.

Nevertheless the legacy of the recently repealed section 28 in England and Wales continues to cause confusion and harm. Teachers are confused about what they can and cannot say and do, and whether they can help pupils who face homophobic bullying and abuse. Local authorities are unclear as to what legitimate services they can provide for lesbian, gay and bisexual members of their communities.

Homophobic bullying

All political parties agree that homophobic bullying is something which needs to be tackled. Following research commissioned by the Stonewall Iris Trust and carried out by London University's Institute of Education, Stonewall's Citizenship 21 project published *Safe for All: a best practice guide to prevent homophobic bullying in secondary schools*.

Sex education

We believe that sex education, like all other teaching, has to be inclusive. The new statutory Sex and Relationship Guidance clearly emphasises stable relationships – some of our fiercest opponents in the Lords have complained that they only mention marriage three times. There is now no excuse for schools to duck the issue or fail to take steps to provide information and guidance on homosexuality.

Education for all

This joint campaign by Stonewall, FFLAG and LGBT Youth Scotland will promote a 'Safe Learning Environment for All' through challenging homophobia and homophobic bullying in education and ensuring accurate information about lesbian, gay and bisexual people and their experiences at all ages. It will create a favourable policy context to address the marginalisation and invisibility that young lesbian, gay and bisexual people have experienced in education. The campaign will be targeted at government, local authorities, schools and the broader education community in order to develop policies, inform attitudes and effect the changes that will enable lesbian, gay and bisexual young people to fulfil their potential. The campaign will rightly tie in with the national policy focus on raising educational standards and ensuring that pupils are included at the forefront of that process.

Action points

If you are a pupil, parent or a school governor in England, Scotland or Wales, check that your school includes homophobic bullying in its anti-bullying policy, and that it follows the good practice guidance set out in *Stand up for us, Don't Suffer in Silence* and *Safe for All*.

■ The above information is from Stonewall. Please visit their Education for All website for further resources and information on Stonewall's campaign to target homophobic bullying in education: www.stonewall.org.uk/educationforall

© Stonewall

Coming out in favour

Sexuality used to be a secret in the workplace, but a new survey celebrates the UK's most gay-friendly firms. Cathryn Janes tracks a welcome change and hears a horror story from the past

First it was women. Then it was black employees. The disabled followed behind. And now the gay community is making headway in the world of work. Stonewall, the gay campaigning organisation, has released the results of its first Corporate Equality Index, showcasing the UK's top 100 employers for lesbian, gay and bisexual employees. The Index ranks employers according to equality policies, as well as on issues such as whether companies had openly gay, lesbian or bisexual employees on their board of directors. It is hot on the heels of the Civil Partnership Act 2004 and one year after the implementation of the 2003 Employment Equality (Sexual Orientation) Regulations.

Top of the Corporate Equality Index stands the British Council with Citigroup, Crédit Suisse First Boston, IBM and Manchester City Council in joint second place. Other big names on the list include Barclays Bank at number 17, B&Q at 43 and the Royal Mail at 52. Alan Wardle, Stonewall spokesman, says, 'This shows that the treatment of gay employees is improving. It's now illegal to discriminate against gay staff, but employers with good sense know that they must go beyond this with policies and actions. People are not surrounded by white, straight men in the outside world so they shouldn't be in the office.'

Traditionally, British employers have some catching up to do. Endless UK surveys and reports reflect gay employees suffering discrimination from name-calling to physical abuse or dismissal. That's why many keep their sexuality secret, making water-cooler conversations about their personal lives increasingly uncomfortable.

Jo is one woman who knows how awkward things can get. Her experience of discrimination at the hands of the Charterhouse Group between 2002 and 2003 was so bad that she'd prefer to remain anonymous. 'I was a senior therapeutic residential social worker,' she says. 'I was discriminated from the start, even though I disclosed my sexuality at the interview. Staff said things like "I don't mind you being gay as long as you don't touch me up" and they decided that I should work with a certain resident because they were gay too.'

Nevertheless, Jo did well, which was when things turned nasty. 'I was accused of being successful because I had done inappropriate things with the resident,' she says. 'Charterhouse suspended me. I was cleared but soon after was sacked. Their excuse was that communications had broken down so they did not want me back. Worryingly, their solicitor said that they knew they had treated me appallingly but that they would do the same thing to a gay man too.'

Thankfully, things are changing. Employers are increasingly realising that this behaviour isn't good for individuals or themselves. According to Stonewall, diversity is something that every business could benefit from. It accepts that discriminatory behaviour can be as conscious as it is accidental but that in the modern workplace, there is no room for either. So it suggests that all organisations check that their policies comply with the law and explain new legislation to all employees. It also encourages environments where gay employees feel safe with consistent recruitment, benefits for same-sex partners and making decisions on merit alone.

Fiona Bartels-Ellis is head of equal opportunities and diversity for the British Council, which holds the top spot of the CEI. 'We are forward-thinking, modern and committed,' she says, 'and that is reflected in our policies. Our employees can see that we care about their welfare within the organisation.' At the British Council, policies cover gender, race and all sexual orientations. 'We include all colleagues from the top down and pay attention to all strands of diversity from the legal to the moral,' says Bartels-Ellis. 'We have gay employees at the highest levels and this shows other gay staff that the opportunities for development are there for them too. It benefits everyone involved.'

And the benefits are many and varied. In the first instance, all employees are made to feel cared for, building increased retention and productivity. Secondly, many companies report improvements in business performance. That's because a diverse workforce reflects the lives of customers and clients who are more likely to use them. Diversity also means creativity because a varied workplace brings greater scope for change and fresh ideas.

Liz Grant has benefited from the positive impact of diversity. She is business development executive for IBM Global Services, number two on the CEI, and she revealed her sexuality 23 years ago. 'It was scary,' she says. 'I was working for IBM in New Zealand and I thought I'd be rejected by colleagues. Yet I saw very little discrimination at all, an enormous relief.' Grant believes that New Zealand is ahead of the UK in terms of gay issues which is why she fared well. However, she faces this situation continuously. 'I now live in the UK and come out every day of my life,' she says. 'When I meet someone new there's a point at which I have to explain that I am a lesbian. This is not just with work colleagues but with clients and partner organisations as well. Luckily my honesty helps them trust me on other issues too.'

She maintains that it is still hard to come out, but says the climate really is changing. 'Work with your human resources manager to create a positive atmosphere,' she suggests. 'Show them what you can offer and help them truly understand what being gay is all about.'

Top 100 – the facts

- Every employer has an equalities policy that includes sexual orientation.

- 13 have openly gay, lesbian or bisexual members on their board of directors.
- 62 have pension schemes that do not discriminate against same-sex couples.
- 60 consult their own lesbian, gay and bisexual staff group.
- 53 have compulsory diversity training for staff.
- 32 advertise for recruits or promote services in the lesbian, gay and bisexual media.
- 51 have sponsored or supported a lesbian, gay or bisexual organisation or event in the past year.

Monitoring employees

Think carefully before you monitor, says TUC

Employers considering establishing how many of their employees are gay and lesbian and how many of these workers might be happy for their workmates to know about their sexuality should think very carefully before embarking on a monitoring exercise, the TUC has warned as it publishes new guidance for unions and employers.

Although the law now prevents gay, lesbian, bisexual and transgender employees from being sacked or treated unfairly because of their sexuality, the TUC says that homophobia and discrimination against gay workers has not disappeared from UK workplaces. So any attempt to monitor employees must be confidential and sensitive, or it could end up causing more problems than it solves, says the TUC.

Publishing the guidelines encouraging unions to talk to employers about carrying out sexual orientation monitoring exercises, the TUC says that any employer keen to find out more about the composition of their workforce should proceed carefully, otherwise there is a danger that rather than enhancing equality at work, the exact opposite will be achieved.

The law does not require employers to monitor their employees for sexual orientation purposes – unlike the obligation to do so on the grounds of race and gender – but the TUC guidelines say that if handled sensibly, finding out more about how many gay people there are in supervisory positions or how many are taking up employee benefits, could help encourage a more understanding and discrimination-free environment at work.

TUC General Secretary Brendan Barber said: 'The law may have changed to give gay and lesbian workers the legal protection they were previously denied, but the homophobic attitudes that have made life a misery for so many are not going to disappear overnight.

'Employers might think that discovering the numbers of gay people in their workforce will help them provide a more pleasant environment in which to work. But unless handled sensitively, any monitoring exercise could be at best a waste of time, and at worse backfire, with staff refusing to answer the questions honestly. Employers and unions need to work closely to establish what is best for their own particular workplace. Our new guidelines should help them do just that.'

When considering whether or not to embark on a sexual orientation monitoring exercise, the TUC guidelines urge employers to:

- Only proceed if they have a lesbian, gay, bisexual and transgender equality policy already in place, and they are clear about why they want to monitor and what they intend to do with the results;
- There needs to be an absolute guarantee of confidentiality of the information collected and that the data remain anomymous;
- The monitoring form needs to make it clear that answering the questions on sexual orientation or gender identity is optional.

- The above information is from the Trades Union Congress' website which can be found at www.tuc.org.uk

Homosexuality in the armed forces

Navy's new message: your country needs you, especially if you are gay. Admirals shed centuries of repression with pink press adverts

It is a liaison that would once have turned many military top brass purple with rage. Five years after the ban on homosexuality in the armed forces was lifted, the Royal Navy is entering into a partnership with Stonewall and actively seeking gay recruits by advertising in the pink press.

Subject to smutty innuendo ever since Churchill supposedly dismissed Britain's naval tradition as 'nothing but rum, sodomy and the lash', the navy will cast off centuries of repression and inhibition by seeking Stonewall's advice on the recruitment and retention of gay and lesbian sailors. In a transformation likened by activists to turning round a supertanker, the navy will pay the pressure group for advice on curbing prejudice and ensuring gay personnel have equal rights to housing, benefits and pensions.

Despite the persistent swirl of sexual rumour around some of Britain's most celebrated war heroes, homosexuality remained the last taboo in the armed forces until 2000, when the government was forced by the European court of human rights to withdraw its ban on homosexuality in the military. Then, Stonewall was the sworn enemy of many admirals and air marshals for taking the case of sacked gay servicemen to the European courts. Openly gay soldiers and sailors have since seen active service in Iraq, but relatively few of the estimated 2,100 gay and lesbian sailors have felt sufficiently relaxed to come out since the ban was lifted. A spokesman for the navy accepted that pockets of prejudice remained and that there was 'room for improvement' but said it was 'committed to establishing a culture and climate where people can discuss their sexual orientation without risk of abuse or intimidation'.

By Patrick Barkham

The partnership with Stonewall 'will help the lesbians and gays within the Royal Navy be more comfortable and honest about their sexuality if they wish to', said the spokesman. 'But no one has to reveal their sexual orientation in the armed services. It's an entirely private matter.'

> *The partnership with Stonewall 'will help the lesbians and gays within the Royal Navy be more comfortable and honest about their sexuality if they wish to'*

There was once a 'dark climate' in the navy, according to Lieutenant Commander Craig Jones, the most senior openly gay officer across all three armed forces. But he was now comfortable taking his partner to official functions and could laugh off jokes about being posted to Baghdad to 'redecorate' the city.

He welcomed the link with Stonewall. 'There is a historical culture of banter in the armed forces. If people are able to acknowledge my sexuality even through a little bit of well-intentioned banter, that's fine. It makes me feel they are comfortable with the fact that I am gay. It requires a certain robustness of character to be in the armed forces but that does not mean you should tolerate anything that is quite clearly inappropriate. In the last five years I've never had to reproach anybody.'

The navy's liaison with Stonewall was kept a closely guarded secret during more than 12 months of negotiations. The group hopes the army and the RAF will follow the navy's incursion into once-forbidden territory.

Ben Summerskill, chief executive of Stonewall, admitted he was

surprised by how far the navy's attitude to homosexuality had shifted in recent years. 'I never thought when I was recruited by Stonewall that I would one day be issuing a media release featuring supportive quotes from the Second Sea Lord.'

He said he anticipated 'up-market saloon bar prejudice' against the partnership, but insisted the navy was not simply 'ticking boxes'.

'The navy would not engage in this process if they did not think there were real organisational benefits. They are not doing it to be touchy feely.' Steve Johnston, chairman of the Armed Forces Lesbian and Gay Association, said he hoped the new advertising campaign and the retirement of implacably homophobic 'old farts' will encourage more gay servicemen and women to be open about their sexuality. Asked to leave the army after his sexuality was investigated in 1990, Mr Johnston called the navy's move 'a major step forward' but said it would also be greeted with sadness by many veterans who needlessly lost their jobs over their sexuality in the past.

'Who would have considered 10 years ago that the navy would be advertising in the pink periodicals? This is all the right moves in all the right directions. Fortunately – and sadly – our work now is less and less because the forces' welfare organisations are taking on our role.'

By signing up to Stonewall's 'diversity champions' programme, the navy joins such organisations as British Airways, IBM and Sainsbury's. Exchanging ideas on equal opportunities in the workplace during 'networking' sessions with such blue-chip companies is part of the partnership, which will be overseen by Vice-Admiral Sir James Burnell-Nugent, the Second Sea Lord.

'I am committed to ensuring the Royal Navy has a culture in which all our people are valued for them-selves and are thus able to give 100% to their job,' he said. 'I look forward to working with Stonewall to help make this happen.'

Queens and country

Lord Kitchener (1850-1916)
He never married and appreciated porcelain, fine fabrics and interior decor, but it is disputed whether Horatio Kitchener was gay or was just more interested in empire than the opposite sex. The hero of Sudan and the Boer war, whose portrait encouraged millions to enlist for the first world war, was declared gay by many historians. Little was known about his sexual preferences, although a contemporary journalist remarked that Kitchener 'has the failing acquired by most of the Egyptian officers, a taste for buggery'.

Richard I (1157-1199)
A towering man and his mother's favourite, the third son of Henry II earned the sobriquet the Lionheart for his campaigns in France and crusades in the Holy Land. He married but never had children.

TE Lawrence (1888-1935)
The novelist and soldier hailed as Lawrence of Arabia was renowned for his heroic role as a British liaison officer during the Arab Revolt of 1916-1918. He was also subject to rumours about other liaisons, particularly after a military colleague said he was hired to give Lawrence masochistic beatings. Poems include dedications to male friends while his writing, including his autobiographical account of his struggle in the Middle East, *Seven Pillars of Wisdom*, also contains richly homoerotic passages.

Alexander the Great (356BC-323BC)
The conqueror of the Persian empire and King of Macedon sported eyeliner and a leather miniskirt in the recent Oliver Stone film, which outraged audiences in the US. Alexander has long been claimed as a gay hero, although controversialists and revisionists have also variously portrayed him as a Freemason, a diabetic, a madman and the inventor of chess.

Field Marshal Montgomery (1887-1976)
Howls of outrage greeted claims by his authorised biographer that Britain's most famous commander in the second world war was a repressed homosexual. According to Nigel Hamilton, Monty, who was married, wrote letters to young boys he befriended betraying his homoerotic urges. Nancy Mitford recorded the surreal experience of meeting Monty at a postwar fashion show in Paris. Revisionist accounts of the lives of war heroes, including Lord Nelson, General Gordon and Robert Baden-Powell, have also made claims that they were homosexual.

Cmdr Jones said there were 'an increasing number of officers who are out and have good experiences of being gay in the armed services'.

'There has been an enormous climate change in the armed forces over the last five years. Many of the admirals, generals and air marshals who were so concerned by this policy change must look back and think "what was all the fuss about?" It has been a total success. We also have hundreds of gay and lesbian personnel who might otherwise have been sacked.

'I do recognise there may be some who have bad experiences. I hope they have the confidence to report it. This is about building the confidence of gay men and women so they can take part in naval society.'

Teens, sex and the law

Frequently asked questions

AVERT
AVERTing HIV & AIDS Worldwide

It seems to many teens that adults are always making a big deal about people having sex under the age of consent. Many young people think that if they feel ready to have sex and they use protection, it is nothing to do with anyone else. But every teen needs to know the laws and what they mean.

So what does the age of consent mean?

The age of consent is the age when the law says you can agree to have sex. Before you reach this age, you can't legally have sex with anyone, however old they are. The law says that to be able to have sex, both partners must be over the age of consent.

But our parents say it's okay. . .

That doesn't make any difference – your parents don't make the law. Teens can't get around the laws for smoking, drinking or driving because their parents say so, and it's the same with this. The age of consent laws always apply, whether you're in love, or you've been together for ages, or you've had sex before.

But it's no one else's business. Why do we have these laws?

Although many young people are mature enough to know how to deal with it if someone tries to get them to have sex, some teens are not grown up enough to know what to do. Age of consent laws are there to stop young people from being exploited by adults.

What is the age of consent?

What the age of consent is depends on where you live – there are different age limits in different places, and in some places the age of consent is different for boys and for girls. To find out about the age of consent in your country or state, please see our age of consent chart.

Is there an age of consent for gay men and lesbians?

Yes. Some places have different age of consent limits for gay men and lesbians, and in other places this sort of relationship is against the law. To find out about your area, check our age of consent chart.

What is 'statutory rape'?

If you are under the age of consent and you choose to have sex with someone who is over the age of consent, then they can be charged with the crime of 'statutory rape'. Some countries have different names for this crime, and some states in the US call it 'unlawful sexual penetration' or just 'rape'.

And what's sexual abuse?

This is when a person under the age of consent is pressured into any type of sexual contact that they do not agree to. If you know anyone who is being pressurised in this way, you should tell an adult what's going on. Telephone helplines in your country should be able to give you advice and information.

■ The above information from AVERT. For more information visit their website at www.avert.org

© AVERT

Age of consent

Country	Male-Female Sex	Male-Male Sex	Female-Female Sex
Austria	14	18	14
Belgium	16/18	16	16
Canada	14	14?/18	14
Cyprus	17	17	17
Denmark	15	15	15
Finland	16	16	16
France	15	15	15
Germany	14/16	14/16	14/16
Greece	15/17	17	15/17
India	16	Illegal	Illegal
Ireland	17	17	17
Netherlands	12/16	12/16	12/16
Norway	16	16	16
Portugal	14/16?	?	?
Spain	13	13	13
Turkey	18	18	18
UK – England, Scotland & Wales	16	16	16
UK – Northern Ireland	17	17	17

Where the symbol ? is used, information is incomplete or unavailable.

Source: AVERT

Gay milestones

The fight for LGB rights over 100 years!

How do we know if the world is changing unless we examine where we came from? The history of the LGBT community is one of inequalities and downright hatred, but things are slowly changing; here are some events in queer history that have shaped the world we live in today.

Twenties

1921: The House of Commons approved a clause making 'Gross Indecency by Females' subject to the same penalties as that between males. The House of Lords, however, rejected the clause on the grounds that it would simply publicise a vice that the overwhelming majority of British women knew nothing about.

1928: A London court action began against Radclyffe Hall's *The Well of Loneliness*, the first major novel written in English with an explicitly pro lesbian theme. Despite protests from intellectuals, and a foreword by a renowned sexologist the book was declared obscene and sales were banned in England. However, a month later, it was published in America, where more than 20,000 copies of the book were sold in the first month, making it a bestseller.

Fifties

On 28th April 1954, the Home Office announced that a special committee (later called the Wolfenden Committee) was to be formed to study the issue of sex Law reform.

On 4th September 1957, the Wolfenden Report was published. It recommended that private con-

sensual sex acts between men aged 21 or older be decriminalised.

Sixties

On 12th May 1960, the first public meeting of the Homosexual Law Reform Society was attended by more than 1,000 people.

On 7th October 1964 the North West Homosexual Law Reform Committee was formed by Alan Horsfall and Colin Harvey. 40 years and still fighting!

On 12th May 1960, the first public meeting of the Homosexual Law Reform Society was attended by more than 1,000 people

---

1967: At long last, on 27 July, the Sexual Offences Act took effect, decriminalising most private sex acts between men aged 21 or over in England and Wales. However, the age of consent for gay men was set at 21 compared to 16 for heterosexual people and lesbians. The unequal age of consent signalled society's disapproval of homosexuality.

1969: 27 June, in America, a chorus line of drag queens and transvestites can-canned into a two-day running battle with police at the Stonewall Inn, Greenwich Village, New York. This event had a global impact on the fight for queer rights, with groups such as the Gay Liberation Front being formed in London a few months later.

Seventies

1972: The fortnightly *Gay News*, the first British gay newspaper, was founded, and the United Kingdom's first Gay Pride March attracting about 2,000 gay men and lesbians to the centre of London. This was a time when the term 'Bi-chic' emerged, with celebrities such as David Bowie and Lou Reed openly outing themselves as being bisexual.

Eighties

1980: The Sexual Offences Act to be extended to include Scotland,

1981: The first bi group in the UK started meeting in London's Heaven nightclub. Meetings got up to about 80 people,

1982: Sexual Offences Act reaches Northern Ireland.

1982: On 4th July Terry Higgins was one of the first people in the UK to die with AIDS aged 37. By naming the Trust after Terry, the founder members of the Terrence Higgins Trust, who were his friends, hoped to personalise and humanise AIDS in a very public way.

1984: On 10th November at a rally held in Rugby in front of a crowd of 1000, the guest speaker calmly announced, 'My name's Chris Smith, I'm the Labour MP for Islington South and Finsbury and I'm gay.' In so doing, he became the first sitting MP in the history of the House of Commons to voluntarily admit to being homosexual.

1987: Conservative MP David Wilshire introduced Clause 28 as an amendment to the Local Government Bill. The proposed amendment sought to make it illegal for local authorities to 'promote homosexuality or ... promote the teaching in any maintained school of the acceptability of homosexuality'.

1988: On 9th January more than 10,000 lesbians and gay men demonstrated their opposition to Clause 28 in a march through central London. On 2nd February three women protested against Clause 28 by swinging on ropes off the public gallery into the chamber of the House of Lords. 29th On February between 15,000 and 20,000 demonstrators take part in a march in Manchester to protest Clause 28. On 9th March Clause 28 of the Local Government Bill was approved by the House of Commons and became Section 28 of the Local Government Act. On 30th April some 30,000 demon-strators marched in London to protest the passage of Section 28. This is still the largest lesbian and gay rally in UK history.

1989: Ian McKellen, Michael Cashman, and dozens of other gay men and lesbians found the Stonewall Group to monitor legislation in Parliament and lobby for equal rights for lesbians and gay men.

Nineties

1990: Peter Tatchell and other gay and lesbian activists found the Direct Action group OUTRAGE! – vowing to begin a campaign of civil disobedience unprecedented in the UK.

1994: The age of consent for sex between men was reduced to 18 by the Criminal Justice and Public Order Act 1994, by an amendment to that Act passed by a large majority in the House of Commons, after exceptionally effective lobbying from Stonewall and other groups. An amendment to equalise the age at 16 in Scotland, England and Wales was at that time rejected by 27 votes.

On 12th April 1998, Peter Tatchell and six other members of the queer rights group OutRage! interrupted the Archbishop of Canterbury's Easter Sunday sermon in Canterbury Cathedral to protest against Dr Carey's support for anti-gay discrimination. The OutRage! activists climbed into the pulpit, holding up placards. Tatchell spoke to the congregation, criticising Dr Carey's opposition to gay and lesbian human rights.

In 1999 the Government introduced a new Sexual Offences Bill equalising the age of consent. Again this passed in the Commons, but was defeated in the Lords. The Government then decided to use the Parliament Act, which gives the Commons power to pass Bills that have been defeated in the Lords

Noughties

In 2000 another Sexual Offences Bill was introduced and when it was again defeated in the Lords the Parliament Act was used to force the bill through and an equal age of consent became law in January 2001. In Scotland the Scottish Parliament voted for an equal age of consent and agreed that the Westminster Bill should extend to Scotland. This decision finally brought the age of consent for both heterosexual and homosexual sex to 16.

On 10 July 2003 the House of Lords voted overwhelmingly to repeal Section 28 of the Local Government Act in England and Wales. This followed a similar massive vote in the House of Commons in March. The repeal of Section 28 had been supported by a coalition of children's organisations, teachers, school governors, local authorities, trade unions, health experts and lesbian, gay and bisexual groups. Section 28 was officially repealed on 17 November 2003. Kent County Council, though, persist in enshrining similar measures in their own bye-laws.

1st Dec 2003: New legislation aiming to protect workers across the EU from discrimination based on sexuality being implemented protecting their lesbian, gay and bisexual employees from discrimination. In the UK, a clause exempting religious organisations caused controversy, with some organisations claiming the overall effect of the laws are undermined.

2004

Sexual diversity threatens to split the 70 million-strong worldwide Anglican Communion. The ongoing row was sparked by the appointment of a gay bishop in the US, as well as the blessing of same-sex relationships by clergy in Canada. Bishops discuss the publication of the Windsor Report, which was intended to calm the row between traditional and conservative members of the faith.

Figures from a newspaper survey suggest that homophobic hate crime rose across the UK by an average of 23%, with statistics in one area increasing by as much as 210%. The poll into 25 of the UK's 50 police forces followed a spate of attacks in London and found that officers were also seeing anti-gay hate crimes across the country, the poll also found that 5 of the 25 forces that responded to the poll did not keep records of homophobic attacks.

2005

February: The UK's first ever LGBT History Month launched in February. The aim of the event is to present positive LGBT images. Modelled on the success of Black History Month organisers hope that schools in particular will be among those to sign up in a bid to counter homophobic bullying.

The Royal Navy announced a new drive towards equality for its lesbian and gay employees, with a host of new initiatives set to modernise and reform the institution.

March: The government revealed its controversial Equality Bill arguing that the establishment of a single equality commission will give more power to lesbian and gay victims of discrimination. It will be the first time sexual orientation will be included in a UK-wide equality body, along with age and religion.

December: The first Civil Partnerships will take place before Christmas 2005. The Act will be the first time that same-sex couples will have legal recognition and similar rights to married heterosexual couples.

■ The above information is from the Lesbian and Gay Foundation. For further information, visit their website which can be found at www.lgf.org.uk Alternatively, see page 41 for their address details.

© Lesbian and Gay Foundation

Equal as partners

Information from Stonewall

Real issues, real lives

'I lived with my partner, Peter, for 35 years. We met as young men and I adored him to the end. At first we were both poor but Peter became very successful. We had a wonderful life, but a year ago, Peter died. He did make a will, but I had to pay 40% on everything he left to me, including the half share of our own home. I got no benefits from his pension. I know I am not as badly off as some, but I feel terribly angry that so much of what we had built together has gone. A heterosexual couple could be married for a week and they would be protected. Why can't a relationship of 35 years be recognised?'

From December 2005, the Civil Partnership Act 2004 will enable lesbian and gay couples to access the same legal rights and responsibilities as heterosexual married couples. This article describes the situation as it was prior to the change in law, sets out the unequal legal and social treatment of same-sex couples, and in doing so, highlights the reasons why this piece of legislation is so important.

The issues

Lesbian, gay and bisexual rights are not just individual rights. Lesbians, gay men and bisexuals, like everyone else, have family lives and, as both the European Convention and the Universal Declaration of Human Rights recognise, the right to family life is a fundamental human right.

While opinions may differ about what form legal recognition of lesbian and gay partnerships should take, what is beyond doubt is that there is a very deep desire for some form of recognition of same-sex relationships.

Being equal as partners extends beyond being able to register and formalise relationships; it extends into areas of public law, intestacy, taxation and inheritance rights and family law.

The problems

Same-sex partnerships are not legally recognised under UK law. Same-sex partners cannot legally marry or register their partnerships. Co-habiting same-sex partners are only recognised by law in a few areas although this is gradually increasing in recent Scottish legislation. As a result, same-sex partners generally do not enjoy rights, responsibilities and protections provided by the law and are discriminated against and disadvantaged compared to married and cohabiting opposite-sex couples.

There are a few local authorities, cities and towns across Great Britain offering commitment ceremonies and partnership registers for same-sex partners. Although they have significant symbolic meaning, these registers do not have legal consequences.

Taxation

Married couples do not have to pay inheritance tax when one of them dies. Same-sex couples have to pay inheritance tax at 40%, on any part of their estate over the value of £250,000. Although this limit seems high, the estimated value of a shared home forms part of an estate. Many people are therefore forced to sell their family home to pay inheritance tax when their loved one dies.

Being equal as partners extends beyond being able to register and formalise relationships; it extends into areas of public law, intestacy, taxation and family law

---

Pensions and social security

Many occupational pension schemes make no provision for surviving same-sex partners to receive survivor benefits, despite the fact that married and unmarried heterosexual couples receive these benefits and that lesbian, gay and bisexual people pay the same contribution as heterosexual people.

The possibility of changing such schemes has been made easier by a change in the Inland Revenue rules. The Inland Revenue has made it clear that same-sex partners can be considered dependants and that the test of financial dependency is a test of interdependency. A growing number of private companies and public sector agencies are now changing their occupational schemes. In effect, lesbians, gay men and bisexuals subsidise heterosexual couples' survival benefits.

With regard to many social security benefits, lesbians, gay men and bisexuals are only entitled to claim individually and their incomes are not aggregated.

Next of kin

Whereas a spouse can register the death of a husband or wife, a same-sex partner can only register the death as a person 'present at the death' or 'the person making funeral arrangements'.

Following a case of *R v Liverpool City Council* (22 October 2002) taken by a 30-year-old woman who had been living with her partner since 1999, the Government agreed that same-sex couples should have the same rights as unmarried heterosexual partners under the Mental Health Act and now can be considered as 'nearest relatives' after six months of living together. Before this case same-sex partners could only be considered as 'nearest relatives' after five years of living together.

Accidents and compensation

The Fatal Accidents Act allows a spouse or an unmarried heterosexual couple who have been living together as 'husband and wife' for a period of two years to claim compensation for the wrongful death of their partner. Same-sex partners have no claim.

The Criminal Injuries Compensation Scheme deals with compensation for victims of crime and from 3 April 2001 the scheme was changed to put same-sex partners who had lived together for two years in the same position as unmarried heterosexual couples. This means that a same-sex partner can claim compensation following his/her partner's wrongful death.

Housing

The case of *Fitzpatrick v Sterling Housing Association* (1999) concerned the rights of a gay man to succeed to a tenancy under the Rent Act 1977. Mr Fitzpatrick succeeded because he was recognised as a family member, but his relationship was not recognised as equal to that of a heterosexual couple living together as husband and wife.

In 2002 the right for same-sex couples to succeed to a tenancy in the event of the death of a partner was established in the case of *Juan Antonio Mendoza v Ahmad Gaidan*. Mr Mendoza had lived with his partner for thirty years, yet when his partner died his landlord refused to recognise their relationship and doubled the rent. Mr Mendoza challenged the landlord's new conditions in court. The Court of Appeal held that references in legislation referring to 'living together as husband and wife' had to be read under the Human Rights Act as including sexual orientation as an 'impermissible ground of discrimination'. As a result Mr Mendoza could rent the house under the same conditions and the Rent Act applies to same-sex partners in the same way as spouses.

This is the first case in which the Court of Appeal has used the Human Rights Act to re-interpret previous legislation relating to lesbian, gay and bisexual equality. In July 2003, the European Court of Human Rights also ruled in the case of *Karner v Austria* that evicting a surviving same-sex partner after the death of the official tenant is a

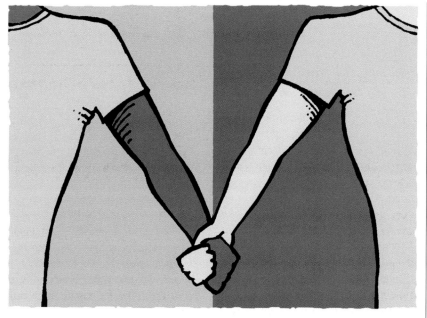

discriminatory violation of the right to a home.

Mr Mendoza's landlord has lost his challenge of the ruling of the Court of Appeal and in its 2004 judgement the House of Lords confirmed that same-sex partners must be recognised under the tenancy law. Recognition of same-sex partners' tenancy succession right is also included in the housing bill.

Immigration

In October 1997 the Unmarried Partners Concession was introduced allowing non-European Union citizens to live in the UK with their partner if the partners have been in a relationship for four years. In June 1999 this period was reduced to two years.

In 1999, following a successful case in the House of Lords, the government amended its instructions to consider claims for asylum by those who feared persecution for being lesbian, gay or bisexual.

Legal aid

In May 2000 the criteria for legal aid were altered to take into account a same-sex partner's income when determining eligibility for legal aid.

Intestacy

The intestacy rules, which govern what happens to someone's estate when they die without leaving a will, make no provision for same-sex partners. Under the Law Reform (Succession) Act 1995 unmarried

heterosexual partners are allowed to make an application for a share of the deceased partner's estate, but the position of same-sex partners was not improved. This means that when someone dies without leaving a will, her/his same-sex partner will not be able to make an application for a share of the deceased partner's estate.

International experience

The only countries in the world that allow same-sex couples to marry are the Netherlands and Belgium, where married same-sex partners obtain all the rights and responsibilities of heterosexual married partners. The only exception in the Netherlands is that same-sex couples cannot adopt a child from abroad. In Belgium, married same-sex couples are not allowed joint adoption. The Canadian provinces of Ontario, British Columbia and Quebec also allow same-sex marriage and the Canadian federal government has proposed to legalise same-sex marriages on a federal level. Same-sex marriage is legal in the US state of Massachusetts. Similar proposals are being discussed in France, Sweden, Spain and Germany.

A number of countries including Denmark, Norway, Sweden, Iceland, France, Germany, Finland, Switzerland, various Spanish provinces, the US states of Vermont and California, and Canada's provinces of Nova Scotia, Quebec, Manitoba, and the Australian state of Tasmania, have introduced registered partnership laws under which same-sex partners may register their relationships and obtain many of the rights and responsibilities of married partners.

Other countries, including the Argentinian provinces of Rio Negro and Buenos Aires City; Brazil; the Australian states of Capital Territory, Queensland, New South Wales, Western Australia and Victoria; Hungary; Croatia; Canada's provinces of Quebec, Ontario, British Columbia, Alberta, Nova Scotia, Manitoba, Saskatchewan and Yukon Territory; the US states of Hawaii, District of Columbia, New Jersey and Connecticut; Portugal and New Zealand, grant same-sex cohabiting couples some or all the rights of cohabiting opposite-sex unmarried partners.

Scotland and Wales

The National Assembly for Wales has no power to legislate in this area. However it is able to do a lot to promote the equal treatment of same-sex couples. In particular, the Lesbian, Gay and Bisexual Forum Cymru asked the Assembly to set up a national civil register where same-sex couples can publicly state their commitment to one another and ensure same-sex partners are recognised as next of kin in the health service.

In Scotland the Adults with Incapacity Act and Housing (Scotland) Act recognise unmarried partners in both heterosexual and gay and lesbian relationships. The Scottish Parliament is looking at extending this recognition to other areas of the law.

Stonewall campaign

Following years of lobbying and campaigning, same-sex partners are already recognised in some areas of law, but there was still a lot of work to be done.

On 30 June 2003, Jacqui Smith, Deputy Minister for Women and Equality, announced a government consultation document proposing legal recognition of same-sex partnerships in England and Wales. According to this proposal, registered same-sex partners would gain a comprehensive range of rights and respons-

ibilities. Similar consultations took place in Scotland and Northern Ireland. On 31 March 2004 the Civil Partnership Bill, proposing the establishment of a civil partnership registration scheme in the UK, was introduced in the House of Lords.

During the report stage members of the House of Lords voted to extend the Bill to family members and carers. This amendment, sponsored by Conservative peer Baroness O'Cathain, made the Bill unworkable and undermined hundreds of years of family law. Stonewall, Carers UK and the Law Society considered that the Bill was the wrong vehicle for such changes. Stonewall has consistently supported protections to family members and

carers but within a separate Bill. The Bill was passed to the House of Commons. The government successfully removed the Lords' amendment. In response to further concerns, the Bill provided full pension equality to same-sex partners.

The bill received royal assent and became law in November 2004. However, it will take another 12 months to implement the Civil Partnership Act and same-sex partners will be able to register from 5 December 2005.

■ The above information is from Stonewall's website which can be found at www.stonewall.org.uk

© Stonewall

Gay servicemen in relationships can live in family quarters

By Jane Mulkerrins

Gay and lesbian personnel in the Armed Forces will be allowed to live in family quarters provided their relationships are registered under the new Civil Partnership Act.

An MoD spokesman said that the new policy would come into effect for all Army, Royal Navy and RAF staff from the autumn. He said: 'If same-sex couples commit themselves to a registered civil partnership that is founded in statute and provides rights and obligations that are comparable to a marriage, the MoD would expect to afford the same recognition in its own policies towards service personnel.'

Anton Hanney, a spokesman for the Navy, said: 'We are obliged to give equal treatment to gay and lesbian partnerships under these terms. They already have equal pension rights.' However, he stressed that the Navy's no-sex policy would remain on ships, at naval bases and in barracks.

The Civil Partnership Act 2004 was passed in November to allow gay and lesbian couples to gain formal legal recognition of their relationship. Civil partners will gain access to a wide range of rights and responsibilities, including employment and pension benefits, fatal accidents compensation and being treated as spouses for all tax purposes.

The Navy has also joined the equal rights charity Stonewall's Diversity Champions Programme to promote the fair treatment of gay, lesbian and bisexual recruits, a first for the Armed Forces. Ben Summerskill, Stonewall's chief executive, said he was optimistic that the Army and the RAF would follow suit. 'I think the Navy have been very courageous to engage with this so publicly,' he said.

Commander Tim Kingsbury, the Navy's diversity and equality policy officer, said: 'Commanding officers have a key role to play in creating a culture in which gay and lesbian personnel feel confident that they work without being harassed or bullied because of their orientation.'

© Telegraph Group Limited, London 2005

Civil Partnership Act 2004

Frequently asked questions

1. General information about civil partnership

What is civil partnership?

Civil partnership is a new legal relationship, which can be formed by two people of the same sex. It gives same-sex couples the ability to obtain legal recognition for their relationship. Couples who form a civil partnership will have a new legal status – that of 'civil partner'.

Same-sex couples who form a civil partnership will have parity of treatment in a wide range of legal matters with those opposite-sex couples who enter into a civil marriage.

The rights and responsibilities civil partners will have include:

- A duty to provide reasonable maintenance for your civil partner and any children of the family;
- Ability to apply for parental responsibility for your civil partner's child;
- Equitable treatment for the purposes of assessment for child support; life assurance; tax, including inheritance tax; employment and pension benefits; inheritance of a tenancy agreement;
- Recognition under intestacy rules;
- Access to fatal accidents compensation;
- Protection from domestic violence; and
- Recognition for immigration and nationality purposes.

When will my partner and I be able to form a civil partnership?

Jacqui Smith MP, the Deputy Minister for Women and Equality, has announced that the Act will come into force on 5 December this year. This will enable the first civil partnerships to be formed under the standard procedure on 21 December.

Why can't we form a civil partnership now?

Bringing the Act into operation involves significant changes in many areas, for example pension legisla-

> *Same-sex couples who form a civil partnership will have parity of treatment in a wide range of legal matters with those opposite-sex couples who enter into a civil marriage*

tion, court rules, immigration rules, the registration service and the benefits agency. There is a considerable amount of secondary legislation to be put before Parliament.

In some cases the introduction of these changes will need to be preceded by a statutory consultation. In others, training of personnel or testing of new systems and procedures will be necessary.

It takes time to make these changes, all of which are critical to the successful implementation of civil partnership.

How does civil partnership differ from marriage?

Civil partnership is a completely new legal relationship, exclusively for same-sex couples, distinct from marriage.

The Government has sought to give civil partners parity of treatment with spouses, as far as is possible, in the rights and responsibilities that flow from forming a civil partnership.

There are a small number of differences between civil partnership and marriage, for example, a civil partnership is formed when the second civil partner signs the relevant document, a civil marriage is formed when the couple exchange spoken words. Opposite-sex couples can opt for a religious or civil marriage ceremony as they choose, whereas formation of a civil partnership will be an exclusively civil procedure.

What are the eligibility requirements for forming a civil partnership?

In order to form a civil partnership in the UK, the couple must both be of the same sex; not already be in a civil partnership or marriage; be 16 years of age or older; and not be within the prohibited degrees of relationship.

In England and Wales and Northern Ireland, individuals who are aged 16 and 17 will have to obtain the written consent of their parent(s) or legal guardian(s) before forming a civil partnership. In Scotland individuals aged 16 or over will be able to register their partnership without the need for parental consent. This is also the rule, in Scotland, for opposite-sex couples who marry.

The prohibited degrees of relationship can be found in Schedule 1 to the Civil Partnership Act for England and Wales, Schedule 10 for Scotland and Schedule 12 for Northern Ireland. These Schedules list the people who, due to the closeness of their relationship with each other, are prohibited from forming a civil partnership with each other or, in certain cases, who are prohibited from forming a civil partnership with each other unless certain conditions are met.

How many people do you expect to form civil partnerships?

The Government expects between 11,000 and 22,000 people to be in a civil partnership by 2010. The full take-up assumptions are available in the final Regulatory Impact Assessment published by the DTI at http://www.dti.gov.uk/access/ria/index.htm#equality

Will I have equal survivor pension rights as a civil partner, i.e. the same as for widowers?

Civil partners will be able to accrue survivor pensions in public service schemes and contracted-out pension schemes from 1988.

What about tax?

Civil partners will be treated in the same way as spouses for tax purposes. These changes will be dealt with in the first available Finance Bill.

2. Forming a civil partnership and dissolution

How would my partner and I go about forming a civil partnership?

A same-sex couple wishing to form a civil partnership will need to visit the registration service to give formal notice in person of their intention to do so.

The Government expects between 11,000 and 22,000 people to be in a civil partnership by 2010

There will be a period of fifteen days between giving this notice and being able to register as civil partners of each other. This will allow the registration service to make the proper checks to ensure that the couple meet the eligibility requirements. If the couple gives notice on different days, the 15-day waiting period is counted from the time that the second of the two notices is given. If an objection is made during the waiting period, the objection will have to be dealt with before the registration can take place.

When the couple give notice, they will be asked to state where they wish their civil partnership

registration to take place. A civil partnership is formed when the proposed civil partners sign the relevant document in the presence of a registration officer and two witnesses. The civil partnership comes into being once the second civil partner signs the document.

Note: there are special procedures for forming a civil partnership when one of the couple is seriously ill and not expected to recover; or is detained in a hospital or prison; or when one of the parties is subject to UK immigration control. Also, different procedures apply for two people who were formerly married to each other, where one of them has changed gender and they wish to quickly form a civil partnership with each other.

Can we have a civil partnership ceremony?

Couples will be able to arrange a ceremony in addition to the registration procedure if they wish, but the Civil Partnership Act does not require a ceremony as part of the registration procedure. Civil partnership registration is an entirely secular process, and the Civil Partnership Act prevents any religious service from taking place during the statutory steps leading to the formation of a civil partnership.

Local authorities will be free to offer a ceremony if they so wish. Whether a ceremony is held will be a decision for the couple, and the local authority, if they are involved.

Will civil partnership be available throughout the UK?

The Civil Partnership Act establishes civil partnership in England and Wales, Scotland and Northern Ireland. The procedures for civil partnership registration and dissolution and the rights and responsibilities flowing from civil partnership in England and Wales can be found in Part 2 of the Act. The comparable provisions for Scotland can be found in Part 3 of the Act and Northern Ireland in Part 4 of the Act.

This reflects the separate legal framework in place in the different parts of the UK. The differences between the different parts of the

UK are mainly of a procedural nature. Any queries about civil partnership in Scotland or Northern Ireland should be directed to the Scottish Executive or to the Office of Law Reform in Northern Ireland.

How will dissolution proceedings work?

Registering as civil partners is a serious commitment, because a civil partnership ends only on formal dissolution or annulment, or on the death of one of the parties.

The process for dissolution will be court-based. The person applying for the partnership to be dissolved will have to provide evidence that the civil partnership has broken down irretrievably.

The dissolution process will begin with an application to the court in the form required by the court rules for civil partnership proceedings.

In order to prove irretrievable breakdown it will be necessary to provide evidence of one or more of the following facts to support the application for dissolution:

- Unreasonable behaviour, that is behaviour such that the applicant cannot reasonably be expected to live with their civil partner;
- Separation for two years, where the other civil partner consents to a dissolution order being made;
- Separation for five years, where the other civil partner does not consent to a dissolution order being made;
- That the other civil partner has deserted the applicant for a period of two years prior to the application.

The court will be required to inquire as far as is possible into the facts alleged by the applicant and into any facts alleged by their civil partner. If the court is satisfied on the evidence that the civil partnership has broken down irretrievably, a dissolution order can be granted.

- The above information is from the DTI's Women and Equality Unit's website which can be found at www.womenandequalityunit.gov.uk

Sexuality, discrimination and the work place

An NUS guide to knowing your rights

Introduction

The Employment Equality (Sexual Orientation) Regulations 2003 outlaw discrimination and harassment at work on the grounds of sexual orientation. These regulations cover: recruitment, pay, working conditions, promotion, dismissal, training and references. This article aims to explain what your rights are in the workplace and what you can do if you have been harassed or discriminated against. If you would like further information on this article or other materials and briefings produced by the National Union of Students Lesbian, Gay and Bisexual Campaign, please e-mail us at: lgb@nus.org.uk

What are the regulations?

The regulations protect people from several kinds of discrimination. These include:

Harassment

Unwanted conduct that violates people's dignity or creates an intimidating, hostile, humiliating or offensive environment.

Direct discrimination

Treating people less favourably than others because of their sexual orientation.

Indirect discrimination

Applying a practice or criteria which disadvantages people of a particular orientation and is not justified in objective terms.

Victimisation

Treating people less favourably because of an action they have taken in connection with the Employment Equality (Sexual Orientation) Regulations 2003. For example, making a complaint or giving evidence at a tribunal.

It is a good idea to try and deal with harassment and discrimination as soon as possible

---

The regulations protect people of all sexual orientations: lesbian, gay, bisexual and heterosexual people both in employment and vocational training. The law also covers perception of sexual orientation; therefore it applies to people who are assumed (rightly or wrongly) to be of a particular sexual orientation. The law also protects people who are discriminated against because of the sexual orientation of those they are associated with, i.e. friends and family.

What to do if you have been harassed or discriminated against

If you have been harassed, it may be a good idea to explain to the person who is harassing you that their behaviour is unacceptable and you would like them to stop. However, you do not need to do this if you are feeling intimidated or threatened.

It is a good idea to try and deal with harassment and discrimination as soon as possible. It may be worth contacting your organisation's human resources department or their equal opportunities representative. Discrimination and harassment can be accidental or unintentional and may be easily sorted out.

If your manager or HR department is unable or unwilling to help you, then you can use your organisation's grievance procedure. You have the right to be accompanied by a colleague or trade union representative to any grievance hearing. If you're not satisfied with the outcome of your grievance procedure then you have a right of appeal.

If you are still not satisfied with the outcome, your organisation does not have a grievance procedure, or you are being intimidated from accessing such a procedure then you may have the basis for a complaint at an Employment Tribunal, relying on the Employment Equality (Sexual Orientation) Regulations 2003. Complaints should be made no later

than three months from the end of the discrimination you are complaining about. Remember that you do not have to have left your job in order to make a complaint.

Where to get help
- Your trade union
- Your manager
- Your HR or personnel department
- Your students' union
- An employment tribunal

Harassment checklist
- Say no – tell your harasser their behaviour is unacceptable
- Speak out – tell your manager or HR department
- Get help – ask your union to help
- Make a record of the harassment – it might be useful later
- Act quickly – remember the three-month deadline from the date of the act complained about to submit a tribunal claim

More information . . .
TUC Worksmart website: www.worksmart.org.uk
ACAS Helpline: 08457 47 47 47
TUC Know Your Rights line: 0870 600 4882

- The above information is from NUS LGB campaign's website. For more information visit the website at www.nusonline.co.uk/campaigns/lgb
© NUS Online

Violent and hate crime

Information from Stonewall

Introduction
Hate crime is very common in the UK. It can destroy lives. This article provides information on how hate crime is defined, what the law says and how common it is.

Definition of hate crime
The Association of Chief Police Officers (ACPO) defines hate crime as 'a crime where the perpetrator's prejudice against any identifiable group of people is a factor in determining who is victimised'.

According to such a broad and inclusive definition, a victim of hate crime does not have to be a member of a minority or someone who is generally considered to be 'vulnerable'. For example, the friends of a visible minority ethnic person, lesbian or refugee may be victimised because of their association.

The Stephen Lawrence Inquiry Report (recommendation 12) defines a racist incident as 'any incident which is perceived to be racist by the victim or any other person'.

The definition of a homophobic incident can be adopted by analogy with the definition of a racist incident: 'any incident which is perceived to be homophobic by the victim or any other person (that is directed to impact on those perceived to be lesbian, gay, bisexual or transgender)'.

When a person who is a member of both BME and LGBT communities is the victim of hate crime, it is up to the victim or any other person to define whether it is a racist or homophobic incident or both.

Domestic violence can be considered a hate crime and some police forces have joint domestic violence and hate crime units.

The law on hate crime
Police forces in most parts of the country are now recording hate crimes and there has been progress:

In 1998 a new offence of racially aggravated assault was introduced.

In 2002 the incitement to racial hatred laws were amended to cover incitement to religious hatred.

Criminal Justice Act 2003 provides increased sentence for assault involving or motivated by hostility based on disability or sexual orientation in England and Wales.

The Criminal Justice Act 2003 does not create an offence for homophobic assault as such. However, it ensures that where an assault involved or was motivated by hostility or prejudice based on disability or sexual orientation (actual or perceived) the judge is required to:
- treat this as an aggravating factor and
- state in open court any extra elements of the sentence that they are giving for the aggravation.

The Criminal Justice Act 2003 does not specify the amount by which sentences should be increased where disability or sexual orientation are aggravating factors. This will be specified in further secondary legislation.

The decision on when each provision of the Act comes into force has not been taken yet and the government currently is assessing the cost and training implications across the criminal justice system.

Similar processes to recognise homophobic assault as 'hate crime' have also started in Northern Ireland. Scottish Executive has published a consultation paper on hate crime to consider what improvements, including legislation, could be made to deal with crimes based on hatred towards social groups. Deadline for this consultation is 30 April 2004.

Community Safety Partnerships

Local authorities have a duty to work with the police to create crime reduction strategies for their area. Statutory guidance to the Crime and Disorder Act 1998 required the police and local authorities to work with and invite the participation of local LGB communities in these Community Safety Partnerships.

The incidence of homophobic hate crime

The bombing of the Admiral Duncan pub in Old Compton Street (April 1999) was a frightening reminder of

the ever-present reality of violent crime against lesbians, gay men and bisexuals.

Indeed, the statistics are alarming. *Queer Bashing*, Stonewall's 1995 study of violence against lesbians and gay men in Britain, found that one in three gay men and one in four lesbians had experienced at least one violent attack during 1990-1995. Because of fear of becoming the victim of homophobic violence, 65% of respondents always or sometimes avoided telling people they were gay, and 59% of respondents always or sometimes tried to avoid looking obviously gay.

The problem is even worse for young lesbians, gay men and bisexuals. For those aged under 18, 48% of respondents had experienced violence, 61% had been harassed and an astonishing 90% had experienced verbal abuse because of their sexuality.

Breaking the Chain of Hate, the National Advisory Group's 1999 national survey examining levels of homophobic crime and community confidence towards the police service, confirmed these statistics:
- 66% of 2,500 respondents stated that they had been a victim of a homophobic incident
- only 18% of all homophobic incidents were reported
- 70% were fearful of reporting future homophobic incidents.

Reasons for not reporting included:
- lack of confidence in the police
- anticipated negative reaction
- fear of being charged with gay offence
- fear of being outed
- fear of retribution
- acceptance of violence and abuse.

A more recent study, *The Low Down, Black Lesbians, Gay Men and Bisexual People talk about their experiences and needs*, by GALOP (2001), the London Gay and Lesbian Policing Group, found similarly high levels of violence and abuse against lesbian and gay black and minority ethnic groups.

68% experienced homophobic abuse and 81% experienced racist abuse. 10% experienced homophobic violence and 24% experienced racist violence.

- The above information is from Stonewall's website which can be found at www.stonewall.org.uk

© *Stonewall*

Homophobic bullying

Experiences of homophobic bullying as reported by 190 LGB men and women

Male | Female

	Male	Female
Name-calling	85%	69%
Public ridicule	75%	54%
Hitting/kicking	68%	31%
Rumour-mongering	57%	67%
Teasing	58%	56%
Frightened by a look/stare	54%	44%
Belongings taken	47%	31%
Social isolation	24%	41%
Sexual assault	13%	5%

Source: (Rivers, 2000) Stand up for us, DFES, DoH. Crown copyright 2004

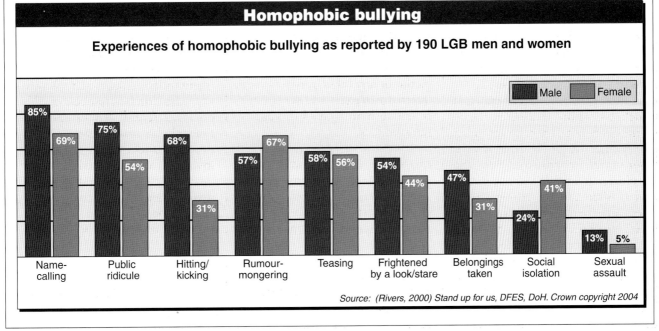

Tackling homophobia

Despite recently experiencing a campaign of homophobic harassment at school, Helen Bowes decided to bite the bullet and 'come out' as bisexual

Helen teaches at Wootton Upper School in Wootton, Bedfordshire. The campaign started when she tried to stop students using 'gay' as a term of abuse. This led to them asking her inappropriate personal questions in lessons and then on to name-calling both in the classroom and outside.

However, employment laws which were passed on 1 December 2003 have made it illegal for employers to discriminate or tolerate discrimination against an employee on the grounds of their perceived or actual sexual orientation.

With an estimated 35,000 lesbian, gay and bisexual (LGB) teachers in England – represented in almost every school – the significance and potential impact of the legislation is huge.

Alan Wardle, director of parliamentary and public affairs at LGB lobbying group Stonewall, says, 'It's the first time LGBs have enjoyed specific legal protection in the workplace, alongside heterosexuals and people who face discrimination because they are transgender. Schools must now start reassessing certain assumptions that might have become culturally ingrained.'

The new laws have certainly helped Helen. 'The legislation gave me the confidence to approach senior management for support, and, thanks to their help, my personal issue seems to be pretty much resolved. My head of year and deputy head supported me, took decisive action and the harassment stopped,' she says.

Spreading the word

'The culture has to be such that the whole school says "no" to homophobia, not just a couple of teachers,' Helen continues. 'So it's vital that all staff, in all schools, are made aware of the new laws and that steps are taken to ensure swift culture change.'

However, many straight and gay teachers are not aware of the

legislation, or that Section 28, which prohibited local authorities from promoting homosexuality, was repealed last autumn and never applied directly to schools or teachers. But if schools want to safeguard themselves against litigation, it's essential they convey the importance of these new laws to staff and that they act quickly, where necessary, to change school procedure and culture.

Alan stresses that the laws shouldn't be seen as a threat. 'A good school will be doing much of this anyway. It's about leadership – about heads sending out clear messages about what is and is not acceptable and putting explicit policies, procedures and practices in place to create a culture of respect. It should be a whole-school approach, integrated into the school's very fabric.'

Sue Sanders of Schools OUT! – an LGB and transgender support, training and lobby group – is an LGB rep on the discussion panels at the series of the Department for Education and Skills' regional anti-bullying conferences. She says there are practical as well as moral reasons for headteachers to take the lead. 'Apart from being fair, treating all employees with respect and consideration also helps a school recruit and retain the best staff,' she says. 'And,' she adds,

'as well as saving the school money, this could now also preserve their reputation, as it's less likely they'd be hauled up in front of tribunals under these new laws.'

The DfES is conducting research into homophobia in schools and its findings will be presented to ministers later this year. It is also exploring how it can work with organisations such as Schools OUT! to help schools tackle these issues, and considering how they are covered in training for teachers and heads.

Around 3,000 teachers will receive training this year on personal, social and health education, which will help them to address issues such as sexual orientation with young people. Materials for tackling homophobic bullying will also soon be available from the Healthy Schools Programme. Homophobic bullying is included in the Anti-bullying Charter and pack (available from the DfES at www.dfes.gov.uk/bullying) and has been raised at anti-bullying conferences across the country.

Promoting equality

Anne Barton, headteacher at Eltham Green Specialist Sports College in south-east London, says she engaged in equality issues long before the new laws arrived. She says it's up to the whole leadership team to promote equality. 'In the past five years, we have had something of a culture change here. We have a more diverse staff now that reflects this.'

Ms Barton adds that a culture of inclusion and breaking down barriers to pupil achievement permeates her entire school. 'I find it hard to single out specific things as it's become so integrated,' she says. 'It's about the whole school learning not to make certain assumptions.'

Whether teachers choose to 'come out' at school is a personal matter, says Chris Lines, who is chair of NASUWT's Equal Opportunities committee. 'The school must now legally support teachers who choose to reveal their sexual identity. On the other hand, it's also no one's business what someone else's sexuality is and the law likewise protects that privacy too.'

Helen has certainly found some benefits to being 'out'. 'It's good to be able to be open to members of staff when you want to,' she says. 'It's stressful when a colleague asks you what you did that weekend and you feel you have to be vague or evasive.

'Though it's normally inappropriate for students to ask about your private life – and vice versa – if I'm teaching sociology or referring to some research I've done on, say, bisexuality, it often makes sense to draw on personal experience and anecdote as other people do,' she continues. 'One should have and feel the freedom to do this should you want to.'

More awareness

Jonathan Charlesworth, of Educational Action Challenging Homophobia (which supports LGB pupils and teachers), agrees, but he believes teachers need advice on what they can say. 'Teachers need guidance on what it's appropriate to say on LGB matters in class and in wider school life. They must be more aware of the new legislation and the protection it offers.'

As for schools managers, Anne says, 'If a head and their team still aren't tackling equality issues in their school, my question is, "Why aren't they?".'

What the legislation means for schools

The Employment Equality (Sexual Orientation) Regulations came into force on 1 December 2003. It is unlawful to discriminate (directly or indirectly) or harass a person in relation to employment or vocational training on the grounds of that person's sexual orientation.

The legislation means schools now risk legal challenge unless they protect staff from:

- 'being treated less favourably than others – at any stage from recruitment to dismissal, including job offers, their terms of employment, benefits, training and other opportunities – because they are, or are presumed to be lesbian, gay or bisexual or because they associate with people who are

- 'being disadvantaged as a group by workplace practice and policy – if they fail to qualify for workplace benefits, for example – because of their sexual orientation

- 'being harassed, however unintentionally, by the homophobic actions or comments of employers or employees ("harassment" means engaging in unwanted conduct which violates, or is intended to violate, a person's dignity, or creates, or is intended to create, a hostile, offensive, intimidating, degrading, or humiliating environment; this could include telling an employee they can't be "out")'

Schools must be aware that:

- 'the regulations apply to all forms of vocational training including teacher training

- 'they must take appropriate action in response to homophobic actions or comments by pupils or any third party entering the school to deliver services

- 'same-sex partners are now entitled to the same advantages and benefits available to heterosexual non-married partners of school employees

- 'benefits currently offered only to married partners will need to be extended to same-sex civil partners if the Civil Partnership

Bill is ratified by Parliament as drafted

- 'the laws apply to faith schools'

Culture change

Practical steps for a more LGB-friendly secondary school

To help ensure workplace culture is compatible with the new legislation, schools should:

- 'internally publicise the fact and significance of the new legislation

- 'stress that Section 28, which prohibited local authorities from promoting homosexuality, was repealed last autumn and never applied to schools or teachers directly

- 'review all practices and policies – notably the equal opportunities policy (EOP) and anti-bullying policy – to ensure that lesbians, gays and bisexuals (LGBs) are explicitly protected or catered for

- 'ensure that PSHE openly and positively covers the whole range of relationship and family unit scenarios

- 'provide ongoing staff training on recognising and tackling homophobia, and leadership training on culture change for head-teachers

- 'advertise for recruits in LGB media and include explicit EOP/inclusion statements in all adverts and application packs; deliver LGB diversity training in all staff inductions

- 'provide positive images of LGB citizens – past and present, famous or otherwise – in relevant contexts

- 'agree how teachers should respond to any pupil who uses words like "gay" abusively

- 'use inclusive imagery and language in posters, school social invitations and newsletters

- 'make sure that email filters don't block LGB-related words

- 'organise LGB interest groups for staff, where relevant, both for support and consultation

- 'review support procedures for LGB staff who wish to "come out"

- 'finally, do not assume that everyone is heterosexual'

- The above information is from DfES's website: www.dfes.gov.uk

■ The most important thing is to be honest with your feelings and see where they take you. (p. 1)

■ Homophobic bullying occurs when someone is the target of verbal, physical or emotional abuse by individuals or groups because they are lesbian or gay (or thought to be by others). (p. 2)

■ As with heterosexual relationships, in England and Wales it is legal for people who are gay and lesbian to have sex once both partners are 16. In Scotland, it is legal for men to have sex with men if both partners are 16. In Northern Ireland, it is legal for men to have sex with men if they are both 17. (p. 3)

■ Homosexuality is unusual but not unnatural. You could draw a parallel with being left-handed. (p. 5)

■ There are no hard data on the number of lesbians, gay men and bisexuals in the UK as no national census has ever asked people to define their sexual orientation. (p. 9)

■ In 1952 almost 4,000 gay men were arrested in this country simply for being gay – many went to prison and many others suffered the indignity (and often permanent physical and psychological damage) of the supposed 'cures', which included lobotomies, aversion therapy and chemical castration. (p. 10)

■ Coming out is the term used for the act of telling another person that you are gay or bisexual. Coming out to yourself – thinking of yourself as gay or bisexual – comes first. (p. 11)

■ The weight of evidence increasingly suggests that homosexuality is genetic. That is, just as random genetic pattern dictates that one member of a family may be blond haired or left handed, so a similar random pattern in the genes will produce a lesbian or gay orientation. (p. 14)

■ The family, we are frequently told, is the very fabric of our society. We may be personally involved with lesbian and gay people in our families, at work or in our social lives. In any of these settings, lesbians and gay men need our understanding, our support, our respect and our love. (p. 17)

■ The government should place a positive duty on all public bodies to promote equality on the grounds of sexuality, as is currently the case on the grounds of race. (p. 20)

■ 'It is up to schools to make sure that the needs of all pupils are met in their programmes. Young people, whatever their developing sexuality, need to feel that sex and relationship education is relevant to them and sensitive to their needs.' (p. 21)

■ Stonewall was set up in 1989 after section 28 was first passed and fought for its repeal for over 10 years. Stonewall successfully campaigned for the House of Commons and the House of Lords to vote for an amendment to the Local Government Bill 2003 that repealed section 28 in England and Wales. (p. 22)

■ It's now illegal to discriminate against gay staff, but employers with good sense know that they must go beyond this with policies and actions. People are not surrounded by white, straight men in the outside world so they shouldn't be in the office. (p. 23)

■ Although the law now prevents gay, lesbian, bisexual and transgender employees from being sacked or treated unfairly because of their sexuality, the TUC says that homophobia and discrimination against gay workers has not disappeared from UK workplaces. (p. 24)

■ The age of consent is the age when the law says you can agree to have sex. Before you reach this age, you can't legally have sex with anyone, however old they are. The law says that to be able to have sex, both partners must be over the age of consent. (p. 27)

■ From December 2005, the Civil Partnership Act 2004 will enable lesbian and gay couples to access the same legal rights and responsibilities as heterosexual married couples. (p. 30)

■ The only countries in the world that allow same-sex couples to marry are the Netherlands and Belgium, where married same-sex partners obtain all the rights and responsibilities of heterosexual married partners. (p. 31)

■ Civil partnership is a completely new legal relationship, exclusively for same-sex couples, distinct from marriage. (p. 33)

■ The Employment Equality (Sexual Orientation) Regulations 2003 outlaw discrimination and harassment at work on the grounds of sexual orientation. (p. 35)

■ The definition of a homophobic incident can be adopted by analogy with the definition of a racist incident: 'any incident which is perceived to be homophobic by the victim or any other person (that is directed to impact on those perceived to be lesbian, gay, bisexual or transgender)'. (p. 36)

You might like to contact the following organisations for further information. Due to the increasing cost of postage, many organisations cannot respond to enquiries unless they receive a stamped, addressed envelope.

Age Concern England
Astral House
1268 London Road
London, SW16 4ER
Tel: 020 8765 7200
Fax: 020 8765 7211
E-mail: ace@ace.org.uk
Website: www.ageconcern.org.uk
Age Concern information line provides a service to older people, their relatives, friends, carers and professionals.

AVERT
4 Brighton Road
Horsham
West Sussex, RH13 5BA
Tel: 01403 210202
Fax: 01403 211001
E-mail: info@avert.org
Website: www.avert.org
AVERT is a leading UK AIDS Education and Medical Research charity. They are responsible for a wide range of education and medical research work. Produce a wide range of free resources on their website.

Brook
Unit 421, Highgate Studios
53-79 Highgate Road
London, NW5 1TL
Tel: 020 7284 6040
Fax: 020 7284 6050
E-mail: admin@brookcentres.org.uk
Website: www.brook.org.uk
Brook is the only national voluntary sector provider of free and confidential sexual health advice and services specifically for young people under 25. Young people can call Brook free and in confidence on 0800 0185 023.

Families and Friends of Lesbians and Gays (FFLAG)
7 York Court
Wilder Street
Bristol, BS2 8HQ
Tel: 01454 852418
E-mail: info@fflag.org.uk
Website: www.fflag.org.uk

Families and Friends of Lesbians and Gays is a continually growing national voluntary organisation and registered charity with more than 40 telephone helplines across the UK and parents' groups which hold regular meetings.

Healthy Gay Scotland
Suite 2 Beaverhall House
27 Beaverhall Road
Edinburgh, EH7 4JE
Tel: 0131 558 3713
E-mail: info@hgscotland.org.uk
Website:
www.healthygayscotland.com
Healthy Gay Scotland is a Scotland-wide HIV health promotion initiative. Healthy Gay Scotland devises and delivers a national programme of work which aims at preventing the spread of HIV among gay and bisexual men.

Lesbian & Gay Christian Movement (LGCM)
Oxford House
Derbyshire Street
London, E2 6HG
Tel/Fax: 020 7739 1249
E-mail: lgcm@lgcm.org.uk
Website: www.lgcm.org.uk
One aim of the Lesbian & Gay Christian Movement is encourage fellowship, friendship, and support among individual lesbian and gay Christians through prayer, study and action. They run a counselling helpline on 020 7739 8134 on Wednesdays and Sundays from 7.00 pm-9.30pm.

Lesbian and Gay Foundation
Unity House
15 Pritchard Street
(off Charles Street)
Manchester, M1 7DA
Tel: 0161 235 8035
Fax: 0161 235 8036
E-mail: info@lgf.org.uk
Website: www.lgf.org.uk
The Lesbian and Gay Foundation aims to promote and develop services and activities which work

towards real and long-term improvements in the health and quality of life for lesbian, gay, bisexual, transvestite and transsexual people. Helpline 0161 235 8000 evenings only. 6-10 pm.

Peer Support Project
PO Box 153
Manchester, M60 1LP
Tel: 0161 274 4664
Fax: 0161 274 4664
E-mail: office@peer-support.org.uk
pspcore.org.uk/index.php
The Peer Support Project provides peer support services for young (15-25) lesbians, gays and bisexuals in Greater Manchester.

Stonewall Lobby Group Ltd
46 Grosvenor Gardens
London, SW1W 0EB
Tel: 020 7881 9440
Fax: 020 7222 0525
E-mail: info@stonewall.org.uk
Website: www.stonewall.org.uk
Works to achieve fully equal legal rights for lesbians and gay men in the UK, by providing information and support for legislators.

Trades Union Congress – Equal Rights Department (TUC)
Congress House
23-28 Great Russell Street
London, WC1B 3LS
Tel: 020 7636 4030
Fax: 020 7636 0632
E-mail: info@tuc.org.uk
Website: www.tuc.org.uk
The TUC is the voice of Britain at work.

YWCA
Clarendon House
52 Cornmarket Street
Oxford, OX1 3EJ
Tel: 01865 304200
Fax: 01865 204805
E-mail: info@ywca.org.uk
Website: www.ywca.org.uk
The YWCA in England and Wales is a force for change for women who are facing discrimination and inequalities of all kinds.

INDEX

ACKNOWLEDGEMENTS

The publisher is grateful for permission to reproduce the following material.

While every care has been taken to trace and acknowledge copyright, the publisher tenders its apology for any accidental infringement or where copyright has proved untraceable. The publisher would be pleased to come to a suitable arrangement in any such case with the rightful owner.

Chapter One: Addressing Sexuality

Exploring your sexuality, © TheSite.org, Sexual orientation, © Brook, Christianity and homosexuality, © Lesbian and Gay Christian Movement, Transvestism and transsexualism, © TheSite.org, Homosexual link to fertility genes, © Telegraph Group Limited, London 2005, Opening doors, © Age Concern England, A guide for young men on coming out, © Healthy Gay Scotland, Coming out, © Peer Support Project, A guide for families and friends of lesbians and gays, © Families and Friends of Lesbians & Gays (FFLAG), Teachers told to promote Gay Pride, © 2005 Associated Newspapers Ltd, 'Pride Not Prejudice' reveals hidden bullying, © YWCA, Where bullying occurs, © Crown copyright is reproduced with the permission of Her Majesty's Stationery Office, It's official – discrimination affects our health, © Lesbian and Gay Foundation, Equal at school, © Stonewall, Coming out in favour, ©

Guardian Newspapers Limited 2005, Monitoring employees, © Trades Union Congress 2005, Homosexuality in the armed forces, © Guardian Newspapers Limited 2005.

Chapter Two: The Legal Aspects

Teens, sex and the law, © AVERT, Age of consent, © AVERT, Gay milestones, © Lesbian and Gay Foundation, Equal as partners, © Stonewall, Gay servicemen in relationships can live in family quarters, © Telegraph Group Limited, London 2005, Civil Partnership Act 2004, © Crown copyright is reproduced with the permission of Her Majesty's Stationery Office, Sexuality, discrimination and the work place, © NUS Online, Violent and hate crime, © Stonewall, Homophobic bullying, © Crown copyright is reproduced with the permission of Her Majesty's Stationery Office, Tackling homophobia, © Crown copyright is reproduced with the permission of Her Majesty's Stationery Office.

Photographs and illustrations:

Pages 1, 12, 25, 33: Simon Kneebone; pages 3, 23: Bev Aisbett; pages 5, 14, 31: Don Hatcher; pages 8, 17, 38: Angelo Madrid; pages 10, 21: Pumpkin House.

Craig Donnellan
Cambridge
April, 2005